Media, Culture and Morality

WITHDRAWN

Major and terrible events are happening in the world. They are daily reported in the media and yet most people seem to remain unmoved and uncaring. Are the media themselves responsible for this lack of care? Meanwhile, thanks to the emergence and popularity of cultural studies, the media are being studied as never before. But why is that study so often trivial and lacking in moral seriousness? Is the discipline of cultural studies part of the problem rather than, as it would have us believe, the answer? This book poses these questions and encourages reflection on why, for example, advertisements for coffee inspire more discussion than do famines. The book takes aim at the empty heart of cultural studies and argues that the study of the media can only be culturally valuable and morally worthwhile if it remembers the lessons taught by sociology. This is an accessible and controversial book which is bound to inspire debate amongst students and commentators on the media.

Keith Tester is Senior Lecturer, in the School of Social and Historical Studies, University of Portsmouth.

Media, Culture and Morality

Keith Tester

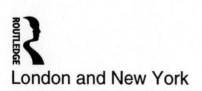

London and New York

First published 1994
by Routledge
11 New Fetter Lane, London EC4 4EE

Simultaneously published in the USA and Canada
by Routledge
29 West 35th Street, New York, NY 10001

Typeset in Times by LaserScript, Mitcham, Surrey
Printed and bound in Great Britain by
Biddles Ltd, Guildford and King's Lynn

British Library Cataloguing in Publication Data
A catalogue record for this book is available from the British Library.

Library of Congress Cataloging in Publication Data has been applied for.

ISBN 0–415–09835–1   ISBN 0–415–09836–X (pbk)

Contents

A
MAGGOT

Introduction

One was, after all, far from wanting to dodge the consequences of having been set down in life under the obligation of admiring this . . . And this transition from finding the things of the world old to finding them beautiful is about the same as that from young people's outlook to the higher moral view-point of adults, which goes on being a ridiculous piece of didacticism until some day, suddenly, one has it oneself.

(Robert Musil)

This book arises out of a sense of incomprehension. The incomprehension runs two ways and revolves around my occupation as a lecturer in sociology and cultural studies. Basically, I do not understand the cultural interests and values of my students and I get the distinct impression that they do not understand mine. We like different things; all we have in common appears to be a dislike of what each other does like. However, this incomprehension is not an entirely personal issue. It represents a more general series of problems and processes which concern the very nature and possibility of the intellectual enterprise of the reflection on culture.

This book is an essay which attempts to unravel and explore some of the reasons for the mutual incomprehension. The book is meant for two main audiences. Firstly, for those who are confused and bewildered like me. I would like to think that this book can offer a little something by way of a support system for the culturally bemused. Secondly, and much more importantly, I intend this book to be read by students in sociology and cultural studies. I would like these students to read this book and, in so doing, spend a little time reflecting *for themselves* on why they like and dislike what they like and dislike. Of course, I am not at all saying that everyone has to uphold the same values as me, but I think it is extremely important that we are able to justify our predilections at a somewhat more sophisticated level than the bland assertion that 'it's good' or 'it's boring'.

I have tried to justify some of my own values through a reflection on the work of writers on questions of culture and morality. Each chapter of this book represents something by way of a critique of the work of others, but I only carry out that critique if it is helpful for the story I want to tell. As such, it is quite wrong to think that this book can be read as a fully comprehensive guide to and discussion of the literature on media and culture. It is not, and in no way does it pretend to be, comprehensive. I have wanted to write in my own voice rather than with the voice of others. This book is more by way of a speculative essay which attempts to develop its own understanding of the nature and implications of the relationships between the media, culture and morality. It is a discussion piece and not a textbook. The book will have exceeded my hopes for it if it stimulates a dialogue that can *demonstrate* and not just *assert* that everything I have said is completely and utterly wrong.

Perhaps my sense of incomprehension is not very original. I do not claim that it is. Ever since critics have been talking about culture they have also been inclined to bemoan what they see as the peculiarities of the generation beneath them. But I want to suggest that the sense of incomprehension I am talking about is much more than a purely generational matter. Although it is important to be extremely cautious about saying that the current era is radically different from any other, it is nevertheless the case that the current situation of cultural and moral value is indeed different from anything known and discussed before. The difference is due to a number of connected factors; inevitably many are centrally concerned with the impact of the growth and establishment of the media. Firstly, cultural production is today dominated by the media to such an extent that no cultural activity or production is untouched by them. Secondly, the media present everything as interesting in and for itself; they tend to utterly destroy the possibility that some things might be qualitatively better than others. Thanks to the media, things tend to be interesting or boring – and that is all they are. Thirdly, and this is the factor which makes the current situation so very different from any other (and which makes this essay rather different from other reflections on the significance of the media), the domination of the media and the collapse of all critical faculties into the categories of the interesting or the boring means that it is not just cultural value that has tended to be destroyed; moral values have been seriously harmed as well.

With the term 'the media' I am referring to the means of communication in social and cultural relationships that do not rely on the face-to-face interaction of individuals. These media are invariably based on electronic or printing technology. For the purposes of this book they are typified by the institutions and the processes associated with such things as the press (that is, newspapers), television, advertising, radio and recorded music. But the main concern of this book is not to explain and explore these different media in and for themselves. Rather, the main concern is to try to understand and appreciate some of the implications for cultural and moral values of these different institutions, technologies and processes.

The word 'value' has two meanings. Firstly, value refers to the qualities of cultural goods (like books, paintings, films, television programmes) which are taken to make them more or less desirable or worthwhile. Here, then, value is about the meanings that are attributed or assigned to objects and activities; the meanings of whether they are civilizing or disgusting, commendable or reprehensible. This meaning of the word value is invariably developed in the debate between high culture and low culture. Secondly, value refers to the moral principles, goals and standards that are upheld by an individual, social class or society. Here, then, value is about the acceptability and appropriateness of an object or activity; it is about whether the object or activity is compatible with or supports the moral standards of the relevant individual or group. In the terms of both the meanings of the word value, however, something can be commended as 'good' or criticized as 'bad'. But the possibility of those reactions presupposes an ability to discriminate and provide justifications and reasoned arguments for why something is so valued. And it is precisely the possibility of this kind of reasoned reflection that the media tend to prejudice.

Contemporary culture is not just one in which it is impossible to provide a reasoned argument for why something is culturally bad. It is also a culture in which it is impossible to say for sure why something like ethnic cleansing in the former Yugoslavia is bad. Indeed, these two different responses of the dull acceptance of what happens might be attributable to the same factors. Moreover, I wish to contend that the debates and subject matters which are conventionally associated with the discipline called cultural studies (and which increasingly enter into the discipline called sociology), are amongst the prime culprits for this state of affairs coming to pass in universities and the media's own reflections on their own impact. Today's students and lecturers now spend all their time and energy talking about Mills & Boon romances or Levi jeans commercials – and meanwhile rape goes on in Bosnia.

Cultural studies is a discipline that is morally cretinous because it is the bastard child of the media it claims to expose. Consequently, the full impact of the media on cultural and moral values can only be appreciated if the study of the media is rescued from the discipline called cultural studies. Note: I am not at all condemning the study of culture as such; my objection is to the debates and the subjects that are associated with the academic discipline called cultural studies. These are two very different things. The study of culture is a valuable, exciting and necessary enterprise. It is also an activity that has a long and highly respectable intellectual pedigree which stretches from Aristotle and Plato to Kant, Hegel, Marx and many others. Cultural studies meanwhile is an institutionalized academic discipline that emerged in Britain in the late 1950s and has become especially identified with a founding moment represented in texts produced by Richard Hoggart, Raymond Williams and Stuart Hall. Through Hall in particular, cultural studies was formalized as a subject matter and mode of inquiry at the University of Birmingham through the 1960s and 1970s. It is through the fall-out from the activities and research of Birmingham's Centre for Contemporary Cultural Studies that cultural studies has been able to claim the study of the media for its own.

But cultural studies pedals a very specific view of the media. In particular, cultural studies has been very concerned to unravel and explore the political dimensions of the media and their texts. This initially involved a remarkable concentration on what is called the ideological dimension of media texts. Meanwhile, during the 1980s the focus of attention became a little less exclusive and cultural studies became concerned to explore some of the pleasures the media can provide. But there is much more to be said about the media than cultural studies can allow. Most of these additional things can be said if a sociological light is brought to bear on the media. This is because sociology holds out the *possibility* of a lively study of culture which is informed by a seriousness of moral and cultural purpose of a kind that is inconceivable from the point of view of cultural studies. (History might have similar possibilities to sociology; but I am not trained as a historian and neither do I teach history. I wish to talk about the world I know best.) This book is written *as if* sociology is such a critique.

Sociology might do this because, unlike cultural studies, if it is worth doing sociology is not happy just to describe and explore what exists. Sociology ought to be driven by a sense of moral commitment and by a moral outrage at what presently passes for the good life; an outrage that cultural studies, with its increasing emphasis on things like clothes and shopping, can say absolutely nothing about.

Sociology ought to seek to know *why* things happen. In so doing it offers the chance that it will be possible to develop an argument for why things ought to have happened differently in the past or could be made to happen differently in the future. Consequently, a sociological approach can mean that we will refuse to take anything at all for granted. Certainly, we will be unable to take it for granted that something is 'good' or 'boring' simply because it is. Sociology can in principle rescue the media – and therefore cultural and moral values – from the trivialization to which they are otherwise all too susceptible.

Zygmunt Bauman has put the same kind of argument about the possibilities and the promises of sociology in a better and a far more concise way. According to Bauman, 'sociology may prompt and encourage us to re-assess our experience' and thus:

> discover many more of its possible interpretations, and to become in the end somewhat more critical, less reconciled to things as they are at present or as we believe them to be (or rather, never consider them not to be).
>
> (Bauman 1990: 16)

It is worth thinking a little about the double negative at the end of this quotation. Bauman is hinting at the tendency we all have to accept some things as so obvious that we become quite unable to imagine what the world would be like without them. These things – such as newspapers and television – become quite trivial to us. Sociology can hold out the promise of a challenge of this tendency. Through the development of what C. Wright Mills famously called a 'sociological imagination' (Mills 1959), it is possible to *defamiliarize the familiar* and, if it is so chosen, *destabilize existing power relations* (Bauman 1990: 15–17). If a sociological imagination is brought to bear on the question of the media and their impact on cultural and moral values, then it is potentially possible to encourage people to think about the media for themselves. People in principle will be able to develop their own attitudes towards the media rather than simply accept what they are told.

As the great German philosopher Martin Heidegger once said, we only know a hammer when it is broken (Heidegger 1962). On the face of it Heidegger's comment is a rather characteristic piece of obscurity, but actually his comment is profound. Heidegger was trying to make the point that a hammer is so much a part of our taken-for-granted and everyday lives that it is used more or less without thinking. We just pick up a hammer and start knocking something into a wall. According to Heidegger, it is only really possible to think about the hammer – consider how it does what it does, examine how it has been made – if the handle snaps or if the head comes flying off. We only know what the hammer does and even actually looks like when it can no longer be taken for granted in the usual way. This book is an essay which uses a sociological imagination to try to break the hammers of, firstly, the dull acceptance of the media and secondly, the appropriation of the study of the media by cultural studies.

In Chapter 1 I will look at the view of the world that has been developed by the discipline of cultural studies. I will show how cultural studies has appropriated the study of the media for itself and has concentrated on popular culture and pleasure in such a way that meaningful questions about cultural and moral value have been at best ignored and at worst pushed quite beyond the asking.

Chapter 2 examines the sociological work on the media associated with Max Horkheimer and, especially, Theodor Adorno. Horkheimer and Adorno are associated with the thesis of the 'culture industry'; I will outline their argument and show how and why they contend that the media tend to destroy all cultural and moral values. Certainly Adorno provides a refreshing antidote to the jollifications and certainties of cultural studies. Chapter 3 looks at the audiences of the media. Adorno in particular had a very definite idea about what the media do to the people who watch and read them. I will outline his position and then show how the view from cultural studies is radically different. In these two chapters I pay so much attention to Adorno and Horkheimer for the simple reason that they offer what might well amount to the most serious, committed and eye-opening sociological appreciation of the impact of the media on cultural and moral values. I want to stress that Chapter 3 is not an encyclopaedic repetition of everything other people have said about the audience. Indeed, the chapter deliberately polarizes the debate about the audience so that the key themes and perspectives in the debate might come out all the more clearly.

With Chapter 4 the focus of the book concentrates much more specifically on moral value. This chapter provides some thoughts on the relationship between the media and morality and it pays attention to how we respond to issues the media identify as moral problems. The possibility that there is a fundamental connection between the media and morality was brought home to me at least in two ways. Firstly, by my own reaction when I see pictures of famine on the television; I invariably say 'Oh dear' and carry on eating my dinner. Secondly, by the work of the philosopher Richard Rorty who has forcefully claimed that television and newspapers are two of the main channels of 'moral progress' in the contemporary world (Rorty 1989). I do not think I am too unusual in my reaction to the images of dreadful things like famines and yet my reaction seems to fly in the face of the point Richard Rorty makes. In Chapter 4 I try to understand and explain this paradox.

Chapter 5 begins to draw in the thread of the preceding discussion. The chapter builds on the themes raised in Chapter 4. In particular, this chapter explores the possibility that the media have produced an audience that is morally and culturally so passive, so uninvolved in questions of value or even responsibility that they are incapable of responding to what they see. The chapter will begin with a brief case study of moral value and moral empathy in the context of media images; I will look at one of Andy Warhol's series of paintings of Jackie Kennedy. The chapter will then discuss the work of Jean Baudrillard who argues that passivity in the face of the media is actually a strategy of politics. The discussion in the book will thus have returned full circle to the kinds of questions that are so important in the narrative of cultural studies. This chapter is also the conclusion to the book.

Obviously, I would hope that the entire book will be read from start to finish as a single entity. However, it is also perfectly possible to read the book as a series of more or less free-standing essays. Ultimately, it is up to you to use the book in whatever way seems most appropriate.

Consequently, this book is something more than just an essay in one version of sociology. It is also an attempt to study some of the ramifications of the media (that is to say; this book is a modest essay in media sociology). Additionally, it can be read as a reflection on the problems and the possibilities of the discipline called cultural studies and as an exploration of the fate of morality in media-dominated milieux. But despite my concerns it should not be thought that I am in any way at all proposing the abolition of cultural studies or for that matter the media. I do not want to abolish cultural studies because in its initial phases (up to about 1984) it managed to revolutionize the nature and horizons of social and cultural research. Cultural studies wonderfully managed to shake out many of the cobwebs of the sociological study of culture. But now cultural studies has its own cobwebs and perhaps it is appropriate for sociology to repay the debt it owes. Secondly, I do not want to abolish the media for the simple reason that Luddism is no longer an attractive political, moral or cultural programme. We have got the media and it is our fate to have to understand them; it is our fate not to be able to wish the media away. The problem is to encourage people to think for themselves about how important the media are; think for ourselves rather than accept what others tell us to think or accept things as inevitable and the way they must be. In that way, the media are more likely to become tools we *might* be able to use for our own ends. *Might . . .*

I owe considerable debts to the people who had to live and work with me whilst I was busy writing this book. I would like to thank Linda Rutherford (again) and Chris Rojek (again) for all their help and understanding.

Chapter 1

The problem of cultural studies

The discipline called cultural studies has had a massive impact on the problems and possibilities of the academic study of culture. It has made new areas of debate leap into the limelight and has transformed the ways in which people tend to look, talk and think about the cultural activities and products that surround them and, indeed, that they perform. Cultural studies has accomplished that rare feat of moving from the small worlds of academia and into the mainstream of informed debate. And it has managed to do all of that in the space of a couple of decades. Without doubt, cultural studies has been one of the greatest success stories of post-war academic and intellectual life, not just in its 'home' of Britain, but increasingly in other parts of the English-speaking world too.

But all of these benefits have associated costs. Perhaps the costs – the dark side of the achievements of cultural studies – could be, or more simply just were, brushed aside during the initial burst of enthusiasm of and for the new discipline. But the costs can be ignored no longer. It is time that they were pulled, if need be screaming and yelling, into the light so that cultural studies can learn to be reflexive, and for that matter, a little more becomingly modest, about all that it has done. I want to propose that the costs associated with cultural studies can be broadly divided into two sorts. Firstly, cultural studies is a discipline built around a narrative theme (the theme of popular culture) which is incapable of sustaining any kind of *critique* of the institutions, arrangements and the practices of everyday life. Secondly, the theme of popular culture is used in such a way that cultural studies becomes incapable of confronting important questions of cultural and moral value in anything approaching a serious manner. Basically, it is reasonable to propose that to the extent that cultural studies has become more and more success-fully involved in the academic and intellectual establishments, so it has become more and more facile and useless if it is hoped to address pressing questions of how we might be required to live as responsible individuals in a world of cultural and moral uncertainty.

Cultural studies has ceased to be a significant and eye-opening study of all that we do and hold dear. Instead, and most certainly since the early 1980s, cultural studies has become little more than a circular, self-validating and exclusive mode of inquiry. Cultural studies has become about nothing other than cultural studies. Within the discipline, certain questions are asked all too repetitively and other questions are asked not at all. In this way it can be suggested that cultural studies has actually become a brake on the study of culture; cultural studies has become an obstacle to be cleared if the study of culture is going to be possible and, moreover, if it is going to be possible in a fashion that makes it *worth* doing.

Cultural studies has become a hindrance rather than a help because it has become increasingly predictable. The predictability has a number of dimensions. Firstly, the predictability surrounds the *mode of address* of cultural studies. Simply, cultural studies texts tend to be written in a very specific language and fashion; a restricted range of references is used to inform the discourse of any number of studies (for example Antonio Gramsci and Raymond Williams are nearly always quoted approvingly) and the language of the texts is indebted to a highly complex and frequently obscure turn of phrase. There is something like a cultural studies house style. Secondly, the predictability surrounds the *objects of study*. Cultural studies texts tend to be about a fairly restricted number of issues: consumerism, the media, sexuality (and more specifically masculinity), the cultural practices of youth. Thirdly, the predictability surrounds the *national focus* of cultural studies. For the most part, cultural studies is about the English-speaking world and, even more specifically, about the experiences of and reactions to metropolitan life in the English-speaking world. Certainly, this Anglocentrism is being rapidly punctured thanks to studies of black cultural forms in the United States and Australia, but one looks generally in vain for a cultural studies light being brought to bear on, say, France or Peru or even Scotland.

Perhaps a fine example of the tendencies that presently bedevil cultural studies is the concern with the study of consumerism. Now, consumerism has always been an important object of scrutiny for cultural studies (for example one of the founding texts of cultural studies – Richard Hoggart's *The Uses of Literacy* – is nothing other than an investigation of the cultural consequences of changing patterns of consumption; see Hoggart 1958), but this object came fully to the fore during the 1980s. The concern with consumption and consumerism reached something like its apotheosis in the pages of the now defunct British magazine *Marxism Today* and, in particular, in the so-called New Times project (see Hall and Jacques 1989). There is little or no sign of an abatement of the concern with consumption and consumerism even though the consumer boom of the 1980s has collapsed into the negative equity recession of the 1990s. Cultural studies work on consumption and consumerism continues to talk about the niche retailing successes of a chain store like Next even though the store and its shoppers have been battered by debt. Moreover, it is perhaps a little immoral to spend scarce academic and intellectual resources on the study of shopping when one of the most obvious facts of the 1990s cultural milieu (at least in Britain) is the collapse of the welfare state. What is interesting about shops today is not what is in them but who sleeps in their doorways. About this cultural studies remains roaringly silent. Indeed, all the time cultural studies continues to be so silent, it will be morally vacuous and, essentially, a wilfully trivial analysis of contemporary social and cultural problems.

It must be stressed that I am in no way blaming the individual practitioners of cultural studies for the silences and the vacuity of what it is that they do. The problems I have identified run much deeper than individual research biographies or interests. The problems are almost necessarily a consequence of the narrative preconditions of the discipline itself. An investigation of the concerns, presuppositions and the procedures of cultural studies shows that the discipline cannot be anything other than silent over questions of cultural and moral value or even certain institutions and arrangements of cultural activity and production. In this chapter I will try to expose some of the preconditions of cultural studies. In so doing I will show how they have involved what amounts to the wholesale appropriation of the study of the media by cultural studies and how that appropriation has, in its turn, led to the development of an immensely peculiar attitude towards what is important about the media. Through all of this revelation, it will eventually be possible to develop some kind of appreciation – or at least a series of vague hints – about how a sociological study of these self-same issues might be not only different but also much more serious.

Any attempt to unravel and reveal the founding assumptions and the narrative procedures of cultural studies is lucky indeed. Not only have the practitioners of the discipline tended to be very keen to talk about the conditions of the emergence of their concerns and perspectives (see, for example, Hall 1980, 1990, 1992) but also cultural studies quickly became a central plank in the academic practices of the Open University. Through this involvement in the distance learning techniques of the Open University, and especially through the clarity and accessibility of the University's course books, the protagonists of cultural studies have outlined their positions very clearly indeed (see, for example, Bennett 1980, 1981, 1981a, 1986, 1986a). However, these texts tend to be of somewhat different kinds. The ones written by Stuart Hall are rather inclined to be histories of the struggles of institutional politics and of different ways of seeing and understanding the world of cultural activity. In Hall's texts, all of these struggles more or less inevitably lead to the carrying out of the kind of work for which cultural studies has become well known. Hall tells tales of a history of Titans. Consequently, his essays might well be revealing and sometimes even almost exciting, but perhaps their usefulness is rather circumscribed; they might well be gold-mines of information for future historians of cultural studies, but perhaps the present moment is too close to the events discussed by Hall to appreciate the full significance of his story (if, of course, significance there is).

For the purposes of this book, and for the purposes of my analysis of cultural studies, the texts produced by Tony Bennett are much more useful. For the most part, Bennett's texts are intended to be either pedagogic in themselves (they are learning aids for the students of the Open University) or they are reflections on pedagogic practices and procedures. Bennett takes great pains to spell out in a clear and concise manner the meanings, implications and what he perceives to be the importance, of cultural studies. As such, it is the work of Tony Bennett that I will mostly use in order to construct a model of the preconditions, directions and indeed the preclusions of the discipline of cultural studies. However, I want to make it plain that I am discussing Bennett's texts in so far as they can be taken to represent the much greater problem of cultural studies; to repeat, my concern is to develop a critique of cultural studies and not the individuals who practise it. It would indeed be possible to say that my use of Bennett is itself something by way of a compliment to his ability to speak for an entire discipline rather than entirely for himself.

Bennett is very careful to define the terms of his discourse. It is important to look at some of these definitions since, to a considerable extent, it is because of definitions of the kinds proposed by Bennett that cultural studies is extraordinarily concerned with some problems and utterly quiet about others. Usefully, Bennett begins at the beginning and defines the meaning of the word 'culture'. Bennett does this because, firstly, culture is a word with a long and complicated history of historical resonances and insinuations (a history that is revealed by a book which is somewhat outside of the canon of cultural studies; Norbert Elias's *The History of Manners*; see Elias 1978); secondly, Bennett has to define the meaning of the word 'culture' because he wants to distance himself from notions that the word can only be applied to certain products like books and paintings but not to others like magazines or photographs. Bennett uses a far larger, and a far more all-encompassing, definition than that. Bennett wants to use the word 'culture' as 'an umbrella term to refer to all of those activities, or practices, which produce sense or meaning' (Bennett 1981: 82). Here, then, Bennett is making a point which not very many sociologists, anthropologists or possibly even philosophers would find it hard to accept. Basically, he is saying that culture consists in all of those things that make our lives and the world make sense. Culture is everything that makes things speak.

But what distinguishes cultural studies from sociology, anthropology or philosophy, is quite what it is that is taken to make sense. Whereas sociologists might concentrate on institutions and arrangements, or where anthropologists might concentrate on ritual practices or strategies of the classification of natural objects, or indeed where philosophers might concentrate on categories of the mind or on some *zeitgeist*, Bennett is more interested in *texts*. Bennett begins modestly, but his definition of culture quickly moves onto more original ground. For him, culture means:

> the customs and rituals that govern or regulate our social relationships on a day-to-day basis as well as those texts – literary, musical, televisual and filmic – through which the social and natural world is re-presented or signified – made meaning of – in particular ways in accordance with particular conventions.
>
> (Bennett 1980: 82–3)

It is worth examining this passage in a little detail and worth trying to take it apart to see how it works.

One of the clearest aspects of Bennett's definition of culture is quite how important he takes culture to be. According to Bennett, it is culture that fundamentally shapes and determines social life. Moreover, for him culture is not something to be found in specific places like art galleries; rather, culture is everywhere and it is everything that we do. Culture is the word processor I am using now just as it is the book you are currently reading. Bennett says that culture is an integral and an indivisible part of our daily lives and, in particular, it is through certain texts which are readily available that the world is made to make sense for us. At this point Bennett's definition of culture begins to hint at the relationships and practices that are at the very heart of the concerns of the cultural studies enterprise. Bennett makes two points which need examination and explanation. Firstly, he says that culture is 'social relationships on a day-to-day basis'. Secondly, he says that the texts which make sense of the world are 'constructed in accordance with particular conventions'. These two points are extremely significant. They lead to the grounding category of the cultural studies narrative; the category of popular culture. They are also the means by which Bennett is able to make his otherwise massively wide definition of culture a little more specific so that it ceases to be 'virtually coterminous with human life. Everything would be in; nothing would be out' (Bennett 1981: 84).

When Bennett says that culture is to be found in day-to-day relationships and that it is also shaped by particular conventions he is basically saying two things. Firstly, Bennett is arguing that culture can only be understood through a detailed analysis of the relationships of the consumption and the production of things like television, literature or films. This would involve detailed studies of institutions and audiences. Secondly, Bennett is making a slightly wider point which suggests that since it is involved in daily life, and since its procedures of production are determined to one degree or another by conventions, so culture has to be analysed in terms of the material and 'real life' relationships which are the basis of the meanings that make the world make sense. Do the meanings come from daily life, which thus simply uses cultural texts as something like blank pages that can in principle make whatever sense we want them to make? Or is meaning a product and a reflection of the conditions of the production of the cultural text and does it thus impose certain definitions on daily life?

These are the two questions, and the two problems to be resolved, which underpin the central cultural studies category of popular culture. Popular culture is understood as the place in which the practices of daily life and the pressures of external conventions come together. For Bennett, popular culture is specifically to be understood as the place of the intersection of the abilities and potentials of daily life to make sense of the world with the capacity of conventions to impose some sense and thereby deny the validity of other senses. This distinction between daily life and outside convention is taken to be one instance of a wider struggle in capitalist social relations. Here, then, when Bennett adds some content to his otherwise broad definitions he tends to provide a very specific inflection to the debate (and a reading of Bennett 1981a at least seems to suggest that the inflection along the lines of the conflicts of capitalist social relationships tends to be based on an assertion as opposed to an analysis). Consequently, Bennett argues that popular culture 'consists not simply of an imposed mass culture that is consonant with the interests of the dominant class, nor simply of a spontaneously oppositional working-class culture' (Bennett 1981a: 31). Instead, popular culture is 'an *area of negotiation* between the two within which – in different forms of popular culture – dominant, subordinate and oppositional elements are "mixed" in different combinations' (Bennett 1981a: 31).

But this negotiation is not at all something that takes place between two equal partners, and neither is it something that is carried out for the benign benefit of all. The point is that this formulation of popular culture means that it almost of necessity becomes identified as a place of complex and pressing political conflict and disputation. For Bennett, it has to be realized that the ruling class does not remain dominant (does not remain the arbiter of convention) solely because it has the big guns of dull compunction at its beck and call. The ruling class remains dominant, and retains dominance, also because it is able to convince other social groups that what is best for it, is, in fact, best for everyone else as well. That is, the ruling class is dominant precisely to the extent that it is able to make itself speak 'for the people'. In this way the word 'popular' is used in a very specific sense; something is popular when it becomes identified as of and for a constituency called 'the people'.

Tony Bennett is making important theoretical points about the status and the implications of popular culture. He is also, of course, seeing popular culture in political terms. After all, if the aim of the ruling class 'is to enjoy social, moral and intellectual authority over the whole of society' (Bennett 1981a: 31), then questions of the consumption and the production of culture, and questions of the negotiations between differently powerful social groups, become political at their very heart. Indeed, Bennett emphasizes the political importance of popular culture – and therefore the centrality of politics to the form and the content of popular culture itself – when he writes that, if the dominant position of the ruling class is to be maintained, 'then its views must reach into and be influential in "framing" the ways in which, at the level of culture, the members of subordinate classes "live", experience or respond to their social situation' (Bennett 1981a: 31). With this comment about the importance of the ideas of the ruling class filtering out to all the other social groups so that the dominated make sense of the world in terms which are not incompatible with the interests of the dominant, Bennett is alluding to the concept of *hegemony*. This concept is absolutely central to the intellectual enterprise of cultural studies. It is also through the concept of hegemony that the practitioners of cultural studies attempted, and for that matter continue to attempt, to link their academic inquiries with practical political matters (and in this way cultural studies upholds the maxim of Karl Marx's 'Eleventh Thesis on Feuerbach' that the point is not just to interpret the world; the point is to change the world as well; see Marx 1946).

Bennett argues that thanks to the concept of hegemony it is possible to examine how, 'within the sphere of popular culture there takes place a series of *transactions* between the culture and ideology of society's ruling groups and those of the subordinate classes' (Bennett 1981a: 31). This theoretical insight itself implies a series of detailed and well-researched studies of the nature of those transactions in the 'real world' of cultural relationships. Bennett continues to say that the transactions between the ruling and the subordinate groups mean that 'through state or commercially provided forms of popular culture, the former [that is, the ruling group] reaches into the latter [that is, the subordinate classes], redefining and re-shaping it only to be partially accepted, opposed, resisted, turned against itself, and so on' (Bennett 1981a: 31). It is important to note the last few words of that last quotation; Bennett is making it quite plain that the ruling class does not establish its rule once and for all so that, after the moment of establishment, it can rest on its laurels. Rather, Bennett is saying that the ruling group has to construct its dominance over and over again, on a day-to-day basis; it can never rest. As such, day-to-day popular culture is itself inevitably a place of conflict, struggle and resistances. But that also means that popular culture is a place of politically motivated compromises and more or less uneasy alliances.

These are all insights which are opened up to cultural studies by the concept of hegemony. The concept is taken from the work of the Italian Marxist philosopher Antonio Gramsci. By the concept of hegemony, Bennett understands 'the processes through which the ruling class seeks to negotiate opposing class cultures onto a cultural and ideological terrain which wins for it a position of leadership' (Bennett 1986: xv). As such, with hegemony the ruling class does not rule to the exclusion of everything that is not of itself but, rather, the ruling class is understood as able to retain its leadership to the extent that it is able to accommodate successfully opposing and competing interests within a general system that is in line with its own interests. Hegemony is about how the ruling class is able to get subordinate social groups to consent to the prevailing state of affairs and it does this by offering the subordinate a stake in the status quo: 'what is thereby consented to is a *negotiated version* of ruling class culture and ideology' (Bennett 1986: xv).

As it were in parenthesis this is a suitable place to point to one of the methodological weaknesses of cultural studies. The quotation from Bennett makes it quite plain that, for him, the ruling class actually indulges in the practices of the construction of hegemony in the 'real world' of social and cultural relationships. But Bennett's texts also use hegemony as a conceptual category. As such, cultural studies can be charged with being guilty of confusing a category of the understanding with a category of material practices; cultural studies might well fall into the trap of blurring the edges between two rather different statuses of the concept of hegemony. Within the narratives of cultural studies, the concept of hegemony is ontologically muddled.

At no place in the *Prison Notebooks*, which is undoubtedly his single most important text, does Gramsci give a sustained and detailed presentation of the meanings and the uses of the concept of hegemony, and indeed the ontological confusion which runs through the cultural studies use of the concept of hegemony is not entirely absent from Gramsci's work either. The confusion over the status of this so important concept is made quite clear when Gramsci comments that 'it must be stressed that the political development of the concept of hegemony represents a great philosophical advance as well as a politico-practical one' (Gramsci 1971: 333). On the one hand, and to give the most favourable gloss on Gramsci's belief, he is making a point about the indivisibility of politics and philosophy. This is clearly a theme which is indebted to the Marxian idea of *praxis*; the unity of theory and practice (a unity which Marx himself was suggesting in the 'Eleventh Thesis on Feuerbach'). But, and on the other hand, it can also be proposed that when Antonio Gramsci makes connections between the philosophical and the political developments of hegemony, he is in fact guilty of blurring the differences and the distinctions between two realms of intellectual activity which, in and of themselves, have no necessary connection. To this extent, it is quite illicit to collapse philosophy into politics as Gramsci rather tended to do in his discussion of hegemony. Within the narratives of cultural studies, the greatest stress is placed on the first of the possible readings of Gramsci's confusion; the reading which stresses the unity of theory and practice. But that is not to deny or even resolve the validity of the second possible reading of Gramsci's muddle.

According to Gramsci (or at least, Gramsci as he evidently wishes to be read – and is read from within cultural studies – as opposed to Gramsci as he might be read), hegemony is the result of a struggle for the leadership of social and cultural forces. A ruling group achieves leadership to the extent that it is able to accommodate or gain the consent of actually or potentially competing groups. As such, a hegemonic group is not necessarily restricted to one class; indeed the logic of the analytic of hegemony indicates that a group will be successful precisely to the extent that it is able to gain the consent of groups from outside of its own class horizons. For Gramsci, a group is hegemonic, and able to reproduce its hegemony, in so far as it brings about 'not only a unison of economic and political aims, but also intellectual and moral unity, posing all the questions . . . on a "universal" plane' (Gramsci 1971: 181–2). This 'universal plane' is that of 'the people' and 'the popular'.

Gramsci continues to draw out some of the implications of this struggle of and for hegemony. He admits that: 'It is true that the State is seen as the organ of one particular group, destined to create favourable conditions for the latter's maximum expansion' (Gramsci 1971: 182). But hegemony consists in the ability of that group to give the subordinate groups a sense that they have something to lose if the existing state of relationships were to collapse: 'But the development and expansion of the particular group are conceived of, and presented, as being the motor force of a universal expansion, of a development of all the "national" energies' (Gramsci 1971: 182). In a sentence, hegemony is about: 'The "spontaneous" consent given by the great masses of the population to the general direction imposed on social life by the dominant fundamental group' (Gramsci 1971: 12). Hegemony shows that what appears to be spontaneous is, in fact, the product of careful and complex political and cultural relationships.

It is precisely this problem of explaining and understanding consent, with the added ingredient of an attempt to explain and understand resistance, which to a very considerable extent drives the cultural studies emphasis on popular culture. Firstly, the cultural studies narrative seeks to explore how and why it is that certain cultural forms are developed and accepted within contemporary social relationships. Secondly, the narrative seeks to explore how it is that the hegemony of the dominant group (a group which, Gramsci stresses, is dominant precisely because 'of its position and function in the world of production'; Gramsci 1971: 12) is developed, and mobilized. Thirdly, cultural studies is in no small part motivated by the assumption that if previous negotiations of hegemony can be revealed, then not only will it be possible to discover how new relationships of hegemony might be practised in the future but also, indeed, how the presently subordinate groups and classes might be able to become integral and dominant parts of a new hegemonic coalition. Fourthly, and as a consequence of the third point in particular, the tendency of cultural studies to be concerned with questions of practical politics means that it tends to adopt a sympathetic – or at least a not entirely critical – attitude towards those cultural practices which it is possible to identify as forms of resistance to the existing relationships of domination and leadership.

A very fine example of the view of the world from the perspective of cultural studies can be found in the book *The Empire Strikes Back*. Undoubtedly, this book, which as its subtitle states is concerned with 'Race and racism in 70s Britain', is fascinating and eye-opening in itself; it is a serious study of serious issues. It stands out as a prime example of what cultural studies was before the discipline became fully institutionalized and established. The book demonstrates the importance of the concept of hegemony to the cultural studies understanding of cultural activity. According to the book, Britain in the 1970s experienced an upsurge of identifications of a 'problem of race' and, as an expression of that upsurge, an increasing deployment of essentially racist themes and ideologies in the interests of the existing ruling forces. This turn to race was understood in terms of a crisis in the political hegemony of the British state. The British state is interpreted as an agent which tried, but failed, to practise hegemony: 'The state has not been totally successful in its attempts to harmonize contradictory social and economic processes' (Solomos, Findlay *et al.* 1982: 18). Indeed, 'it is important to see that the crisis which Britain faced during the seventies, and faces today, is a crisis of hegemony' (Solomos, Findlay *et al.* 1982: 19). Within the crisis, the forces that are struggling to retain their hegemony will play the cards of race and racism precisely because they are seen as ways in which the existing ruling groups can argue that they are behaving in the best interests of a universal constituency of 'the people' called Britain (or, more specifically, the best interests of England).

Within this interpretation of social and political relationships through the concept of hegemony, cultural relationships become extremely important. Not only does the cultural realm become a site of political dispute since it is here that the ruling groups are able to play on and exacerbate racist ideologies (for an incisive analysis of this aspect of the issue see Lawrence 1982), but, and for Paul Gilroy much more importantly, culture becomes the place where the strategies of the ruling groups can be resisted. Culture and politics become associated if not, in some ways, virtually identical. After all, there is held to be a connection between 'the cultural politics of "black" people in this country, and the implications of their struggles for the institutions and practices of the British workers' movement. It is about *class* struggle' (Gilroy 1982: 276). As such, the resistances of 'black people' and the linkages between those cultural forms (such as Rastafarianism) and the 'workers' movement' are also about the meaning of the *popular* in so far as the popular is here understood to refer to that which is of and for the people.

Bennett argues that '"Hegemony" makes it possible to conceptualise such a site [that is, such a site as popular culture] in terms of the business – the production of consent and the construction of popular alliances – conducted upon it' (Bennett 1980: 25). Yet this popular culture is not a thing (it is not something towards which it is possible to point a finger and say 'there it is'). This realization is another of the implications of the concern to explore the relationships of the construction and the main-tenance of the leadership of the ruling groups. Rather than being a 'thing', popular culture is understood as only constituted in and through the complex negotiations and resistances of the never-ending struggles for hegemony. It is a relational field. This has led Tony Bennett at least to make the claim that 'There is no such thing as popular culture' (Bennett 1980: 28). Bennett says that there is no such thing as popular culture precisely because a thing is an object which can be seen as it were 'out there', whereas popular culture is a living milieu of subjective meanings, practices and relationships which is incapable of becoming a stable object. Popular culture, to quote Bennett again, is 'not a specific set of cultural forms and practices but a network of relationships that is differentially filled by different forms and practices at different times' (Bennett 1980: 25). Furthermore, popular culture 'is defined not by those forms and practices which, contingently, happen to fill it at a particular moment but by the processes, exchanges and transactions which take place in, about and across such forms and practices' (Bennett 1980: 25. Compare with Bennett 1986a: 8).

According to the view from cultural studies then, popular culture is a vague but crucial analytic category. The vagueness and importance are similarly attributable to the status of popular culture as a space which does not just exist unproblematically but which has to be created, maintained and defended on a perpetual basis. In these terms, then, popular culture is not just a subject for books; it is also an incitement to practical political action. The narratives and the institutional procedures of cultural studies have indeed tried to develop this possibility of practical political action. Indeed, perhaps this is yet another of the reasons for the initial success and challenge of cultural studies. While people like sociologists were sitting around trying to make their models of social mobility subtle enough to take into account the latest census statistics, the practitioners of cultural studies were urging people to study living cultural practices, the lived realities of oppression and, more importantly, do something about it.

Cultural studies consequently became a means and a training centre for the cadres of the new cultural politics of the resistances and con-structions of hegemony. As Stuart Hall has succinctly said, 'there is no doubt in my mind that we were trying to find an institutional practice in cultural studies that might produce an organic intellectual' (Hall 1992: 281). Like the concept of hegemony, the phrase 'organic intellectual' also comes from the work of Antonio Gramsci. In the *Prison Notebooks*, Gramsci defines organic intellectuals as those intellectuals who are connected to a social group or class. Indeed, Gramsci speculates that 'it should be possible . . . to measure the "organic quality" . . . of the various intellectual strata and their degree of connection with a funda-mental social group' (Gramsci 1971: 12). The role of these organic intellectuals is not simply to connect themselves with a social group but, much more importantly in terms of the struggles of hegemony, the organic intellectuals are responsible for enabling the 'fundamental social group' to attain some kind of political, social and cultural self-awareness. In that way, the organic intellectuals are both the producers and the product of social-political interests: 'there does not exist any independent class of intellectuals, but every social group has its own stratum of intellectuals, or tends to form one' (Gramsci 1971: 60).

But these groups of organic intellectuals do not exist in isolation from each other. On the contrary, they are seen by Gramsci to be the vanguard of the attempt to construct new hegemonies which are able to represent and embody the interests of different arrangements and negotiations of social groups than presently prevail. And in this struggle, the organic intellectuals who speak in the name of the presently oppressed social groups will be the most attractive. As Gramsci puts it: 'the intellectuals of the historically (and concretely) progressive class, in the given conditions, exercise such a power of attraction that, in the last analysis, they end up by subjugating the intellectuals of the other social groups' (Gramsci 1971: 60). In other words, the organic intellectuals are at the forefront of the struggles to speak for and on behalf of the people (and therefore the organic intellectuals are the speakers in the name of the popular).

According to Stuart Hall, Gramsci's notion of the organic intellectual played a highly significant part in the definition of what cultural studies was to be and be about. Certainly Hall takes up Gramsci to validate what he sees as two key aspects of the work of cultural studies. Firstly, Hall uses Gramsci to justify the claim that cultural studies, if it was to be able to produce organic intellectuals, had to be 'at the very forefront of intellectual theoretical work' (Hall 1992: 281). After all, 'If you are in the game of hegemony you have to be smarter than "them." Hence there are no theoretical limits from which cultural studies can turn back' (Hall 1992: 281). Secondly, Hall uses Gramsci to make a point about the responsibility of these organic intellectuals. Hall's argument is that cultural studies is not something that is carried out in seminar rooms for the sake of academic careers; rather cultural studies has a responsibility to become a force to be reckoned with in the material world of day-to-day relationships, day-to-day oppression and the lived experiences of struggles of hegemony. The organic intellectual has a political obligation to communicate her or his work to those social groups with whom there is the organic relationship. As Hall says: 'the organic intellectual cannot absolve himself or herself from the responsibility of transmitting those ideas, that knowledge, through the intellectual function, to those who do not belong, professionally, in the intellectual class' (Hall 1992: 281).

But Hall himself was aware that despite these very enervating intentions, cultural studies was stuck on the horns of a rather basic and extremely embarrassing dilemma. It is one thing to produce organic intellectuals, but it is quite something else for there to be something for all of those intellectuals to be organic to. Hall puts the problem this way:

> The problem about the concept of an organic intellectual is that it appears to align intellectuals with an emerging historic movement and we couldn't tell then, and can hardly tell now, where that emerging historical movement was to be found.
>
> (Hall 1992: 281)

More pithily: 'we were organic intellectuals without any organic point of reference' (Hall 1992: 281).

This is a most fundamental difficulty. The practitioners of cultural studies were turning themselves into organic intellectuals but they were plagued by the problem that quite simply the world would not listen. This kind of difficulty can be read into Paul Gilroy's essay on the cultural politics of 'race' in *The Empire Strikes Back*. Gilroy's essay is motivated by a very powerful and engaging statement of the political insights and strategic lessons that can be learnt from intellectual cultural-studies-type activity by those involved in practical politics. But when Gilroy talks about the cultures of resistance to hegemony and racism which are developed by black youth, he talks about them as if they are things 'out there', as if they are things which are to some extent divorced from the pages of the erstwhile organic texts (see Gilroy 1982).

This problem of who the organic intellectuals are organic to, for and with is resolved by Tony Bennett. For Bennett, the organic intellectuals produced through cultural studies have a responsibility towards 'the people'. But this constituency does not exist 'out there'; rather 'the people' is a group and an identity which is only constructed in and through the struggles and the strategies of popular culture (once again, it is clear that the dominant cultural studies interpretation of the word 'popular' refers to 'of the people'). Consequently, the organic intellec-tuals who study popular culture are not just carrying out intellectual work; they are, much more significantly, revealing the implication of hegemonic struggle in daily life and, thereby, enabling the identification and the construction of a new constituency of 'the people' which is built on the experiences of the presently oppressed groups. As Bennett says in a somewhat ringing phrase, which is a political manifesto and an intellectual methodology at one and the same time: 'The point is not to define "the people" but to *make* them' (Bennett 1986a: 20). Bennett continues to draw out the point of the simultaneously intellectual and practical work of cultural studies. It is 'to make that construction of "the people" which unites a broad alliance of social forces in opposition to the power bloc count politically by winning for it a cultural weight and influence which prevails above others' (Bennett 1986a: 20). If a suitable constituency of 'the people' cannot be found, then Bennett is saying that it will have to be made.

In other words, cultural studies makes itself an organic enterprise, linking theory and practice, precisely because it *invents* (makes rather than finds) that group with which it has an organic relationship. Outside of the cultural studies invention of 'the people' that group does not exist (just as Bennett denied that popular culture can be defined as a thing independently of the struggles of hegemony which constitute it). Popular culture is the culture of 'the people', but in so far as popular culture is not a thing which can be defined through finger-pointing exercises, neither, therefore is 'the people'. They are both whatever cultural studies wills them to be. Indeed, 'attempts to define popular culture by filling it with a particular content . . . closes in on a particular construction of "the people" which . . . stands in a pre-given relationship to that culture' (Bennett 1986a: 18). The point of view from within cultural studies sees the world and its relationships as much more fluid than those kinds of firm and fixed definitions can possibly allow.

It is this combination of intellectual and practical questions which is the basic reason why cultural studies has come to be obsessed and associated with some objects of inquiry as opposed to others. Since cultural studies seeks to understand and help to build a popular culture which is both of and for the people, it tends to be overwhelmingly concerned to explore and unravel the cultural activities that are carried out by that constituency, which can presently be labelled as 'the people'. Firstly, cultural studies has been concerned to explore those aspects of cultural meaning and activity which were previously denigrated by academic commentators on the grounds that they were in some way 'low' or 'uncivilized'. As Stuart Hall has usefully said, cultural studies was and remains, 'primarily concerned with "neglected" materials drawn from popular culture and the mass media, which . . . provided important evidence of the new stresses and directions of contemporary culture' (Hall 1980: 21). Secondly, cultural studies is concerned to explore what popular culture means *now* so that it can appreciate all the better how a new constituency of 'the people' might be constructed in the future. To this extent, and with the assertion that it 'strikes me as exactly right', Tony Bennett has approvingly quoted a passage from the editorial in the first edition of the journal *New Left Review* which stated: 'The task of socialism today is to meet people where they *are*, where they are touched, bitten, moved, frustrated, nauseated' (quoted in Bennett 1986a: 10).

This is the basis of the appropriation of the study of the media by cultural studies. The discipline has always been centrally concerned to explore some of the pleasures and the problems of the media because the media are absolutely central to popular culture. The media are where the people are at; the media are the place where the organic intellectuals must enter into the plays of hegemony in order to construct a new 'people', a new popular culture. Of course, to a large extent the appropriation of the media was made somewhat easier by the fact that, during the 1960s and 1970s sociology hardly screamed and shouted to prevent the baby being taken from its arms. It is probably the case that had cultural studies not taken the study of the media for itself, sociology would have allowed it – by neglect rather than malice aforethought – to wither on the intellectual vine (just as the sociology of religion has been allowed to wither somewhat more recently).

Indeed, the cultural studies annexation of the study of the media has been made all the more easy because the phrase 'popular culture' does not have to be understood only in the way favoured by writers like Tony

Bennett and Stuart Hall. Popular has meanings other than simply 'of the people'. Popular can also mean 'liked by many'. And the media are, indeed, liked – or at the very least actively tolerated – by the many. This definition of popular culture is important in the work of John Fiske. Certainly, it would be quite wrong to say that Fiske is forgetful of the kinds of political concerns that are so vitally important to the other practitioners of cultural studies. Fiske remembers that 'popular culture is formed always in reaction to, and never as part of, the forces of domination' (Fiske 1989: 43). To this extent Fiske rather tends to elide the two different meanings of the word 'popular'; sometimes it is hard to know which definition he is using at a given moment or whether, indeed, he is deliberately trying to use these two rather different meanings of the word 'popular' at one and the same time. This is a problem with the concepts Fiske develops and uses, a problem which he compounds rather than explains in his work.

It would seem to be the case that despite his awareness of the political connotations of the word 'popular', Fiske is far more concerned to emphasize those aspects of popular culture which make certain products and activities pleasurable and liked by many people. For Fiske, it is not only true to say that 'Everyday life is constituted by the practices of popular culture, and is characterized by the creativity of the weak in using the resources provided by a disempowering system while refusing finally to submit to that power' (Fiske 1989: 47). It is also true to say that: 'these clashes of social interests . . . are motivated primarily by pleasure: the pleasure of producing one's own meanings of social experience and the pleasures of avoiding the social discipline of the power-bloc' (Fiske 1989: 47). Struggle is fun. Put another way, and to repeat the ambiguity of Fiske's use of the word 'popular', it might well be said that his work seeks to stress the possibility that it is popular to be popular. This, in turn, implies a small distance between the likes of Hall and Bennett on the one hand and Fiske on the other. Whereas Bennett (explicitly) and Hall (implicitly) identify the 'popular' as something which is definitionally vague because it is not a thing prior to the practices and hegemonic struggles that constitute it, John Fiske is far more inclined to invest the category of the popular with a thing-like 'out there-ness'. As Fiske explains, 'The differences that I call popular are produced by and for the various formations of the people: they oppose and disrupt the organized disciplined individualities produced by the mechanisms of surveillance, examination and information' (Fiske 1992: 161). It is improbable in terms of their own work that Hall and Bennett should want to support that kind of fairly definite definition.

One thing is clear: cultural studies as a discipline is irrevocably harnessed to an agenda of the politics of popular culture. That politics turns two ways. Firstly, it turns around an analytic strategy of the revelation of the relationships between hegemony and popular cultural forms. Secondly, it turns around a practical commitment to the development through organic intellectual activity of a new and a more democratic constituency of the people. As such, cultural studies is a study in the service of changing the world in the interests of those who are presently oppressed. Undoubtedly, it is the enthusiasm and the sincerity of much of that commitment which goes a very long way towards explaining much of the initial appeal of the discipline. But this close connection with a political agenda has led cultural studies to emerge as a narrative with a number of silences and blind-spots. The silences involve a tendency to underplay the importance of some of the less than entirely democratic and laudable activities and practices which are carried out by the presently oppressed (things that are done within the realm of popular culture). The blind-spots are expressions of the preconditions of the very narrative of cultural studies; quite simply, there are some things that cultural studies is structurally incapable of discussing because, if they were opened up to critical investigation, cultural studies would itself become impossible.

A fine example of the kinds of silences that can emerge as a product of the commitment to a political agenda is to be found in some of the work of Paul Willis. Particularly important in this respect is Willis's *Learning to Labour* (Willis 1977). The book is a study of working-class 'lads' in the moment of their transition from school to work. The book is structured around an analysis of interviews with the lads; Willis wants to understand the cultural assumptions and meanings which turn the lads from schoolboys and into more or less compliant members of the working class. One of the things that Willis discovers is the centrality of racism to the lads' culture. Clearly, racism is a set of meanings and practices that has no place in any popular culture which is claimed to be democratic. Neither is it a terribly flattering reflection on the present-day culture of the working class. However, because of the political agenda which informs his work, Willis tends to be rather silent about this undoubtedly popular (in both senses of that word) racism. Indeed, when Willis does discuss it, he transforms his lads from the active makers of their own valuable culture and into the dupes of capitalist hegemony (Willis 1977: 150–3). The problem with Willis' study is that he is incapable of launching any kind of sustained and meaningful *critique* of working-class racism precisely because this racism is an attribute of an oppressed group and, therefore, it *must* be in some way a potential source of antagonism and resistance towards the existing relationships of hegemony. It would rather seem to be the case that principle flies out of the window if it runs counter to the interests of politics.

Similarly, and extremely surprisingly, the issue of working-class racism does not have a terribly strong presence in the pages of *The Empire Strikes Back*. Certainly, that text says a great deal of great interest about the relationships between racist ideologies and hegemonic constructions of 'the nation' and 'the people', but the precise problem of the implication of this ideology in the working class (or indeed the implication of the working class in the construction of the ideology of racism) is barely mentioned. The most useful encounter with working-class racism is made by Errol Lawrence. But even he seems to want to excuse the working class for their ways. For Lawrence, 'the more developed racist ideologies *are popular* precisely because they succeed in reorganizing the common-sense racist ideologies of the white working class, around the themes of "the British nation", "the British people" and "British culture"' (Lawrence 1982: 48). (Of course, when Lawrence uses the phrase 'common-sense' he is using it in a technical fashion after Gramsci. In the *Prison Notebooks*, Gramsci quickly defines common sense as, 'the traditional popular conception of the world – what is unimaginatively called "instinct", although it too is in fact a primitive and elementary historical acquisition' (Gramsci 1971: 199).)

Lawrence is making an interesting analytic point but nevertheless his identification of the appeal of racist ideologies still, in a somewhat central way, excuses the working class for certain of their cultural forms and meanings. For Lawrence, the working class might well uphold racist concepts, but working-class racism operates only at the level of common sense; the working-class attitudes require 'reorganization' if they are to become the kinds of 'more developed' racism that concern Lawrence. As such, Lawrence is implying *either* that the working class might practise and uphold some dubious cultural concepts and meanings, but they are not as dubious as the meanings developed and promoted by the state; *or* he is implying that the working class is little more than the dupe of the forces of hegemony. In either case, what the working class do is made understandable (or at least less important than something else).

Within the limits and the discursive foundations of the narrative of cultural studies, it is impossible to develop any kind of principled moral objection to certain cultural forms. The nature of cultural studies means that moral or cultural value is collapsed more or less entirely into the pragmatic problem of political expediency. A cultural form is oppressive or popular and that is all it is (for an example of the silence of cultural studies over questions of the *acceptability* of certain popular cultural forms, see Malcolmson 1982). As such, there can be, for example, no *necessary principled* objection to a form like working-class racism. Certainly, there can be *political* or *pragmatic* objections, but their moral seriousness will be questionable to say the least. All the time cultural studies continues to be tied to a politics of popular culture, it can have no important moral dimension. It cannot be a serious study since it cannot offer any critique of what presently prevails. All it can do is urge that the presently existing ingredients are mixed into a better cake of hegemony in the future.

From a more explicitly sociological point of view, it could be suggested that the silences of cultural studies are not, in themselves, too difficult to overcome. All that is needed is a political platform built upon a few well-chosen and non-negotiable moral precepts. But the blind-spots are a rather different matter. The problem is this: cultural studies actually *cannot* (rather than, as Bennett argues basically on the grounds of political strategy, *should* not) have any concept of popular culture. The indefinability of popular culture (its lack of a thing-like quality) is not a strategic decision. It is actually a structural weakness in the presuppositions of the discipline of cultural studies. *Cultural studies can have no concept of popular culture.*

As soon as an attempt is made within cultural studies to talk about popular culture, the terms of the debate rather quickly change to emphasize something else. The discussions which present themselves as about popular culture are actually about different relationships and concepts; those of hegemony or pleasure. This slip of the analytic eye is not just a reflection of a situation in which popular culture does not exist outside of the plays of hegemony and pleasure. It is about much more than the possibility that, if the meanings of popular culture are deconstructed (taken apart, examined and put back together again in a new configuration), then all that remains is hegemony and/or pleasure. The blind-spot is, instead, a reflection of a situation in which popular culture is the preconception of cultural studies and that, therefore, cultural studies cannot deconstruct the meaning of popular culture without at the same time deconstructing the meaning and the possibility of itself.

From the point of view that has developed within the narrative of cultural studies, popular culture can be described and constructed as a theoretical-political space, but it cannot be explored in any meaningful way as a space or site of cultural activity and meaning. The products and the activities of popular culture constitute and provide the taken-for-granted presuppositions of cultural studies. Cultural studies identifies itself as an examination of where 'the people are at'. The people are in front of television screens, reading newspapers or listening to music at home. If those activities were themselves bracketed off from the things to be investigated or if, indeed, those media-related activities were shown to be, for the sake of argument, utterly vacuous and little more than a distraction so that we do not get bored before we die, then it would be impossible to have any awareness of this place where the people might be at. Consequently, there would be nothing for cultural studies to talk about. If cultural studies does not take media-related cultural activity entirely for granted, and if it did not presuppose the importance of the media as cultural forms and as providers of meaning, then its discourse would collapse. To this extent, then, cultural studies is indeed a child of the media; a child which cannot will the death of its parents.

This has major consequences. It means that from the point of view of cultural studies, the media, just like other forms and activities of popular culture, cannot possibly be opened up to any sort of critique. The media can be described and challenged on the basis of their implication in the construction of relationships of hegemony, but the existence of the media themselves cannot be doubted. Neither can any significant doubt be entertained as to the desirability of the media. Questions of desirability or value are outside of the agenda of issues that cultural studies can possibly address. All cultural studies can offer is a political criticism (which is, however, tempered by the unquestioned assumption that the media can be better than they are now; the problem is thus held to be one of the *organization* and *operation* of the media as opposed to the media *as such*) or a mindless reverie in the allegedly rich and diverse meanings which are constructed by television or 'on the streets' and which are thus read as the harbingers of new forms of popular culture. Cultural critique is reduced to the simple dichotomy of something being labelled 'boring' or 'good'. No other values – no values such as moral desirability or the promotion of solidarity amongst individuals, and certainly nothing at all like the possibility of the spiritual content of cultural forms – can possibly be entertained from the perspective of cultural studies. Something is, is not or can be popular; that is all there is to be said (indeed that is all there is that can be said).

Certainly, the view from cultural studies perceives a world of immense political complexity and significance. The concept of hegemony is indeed, in its own terms at least, able to identify peaks and troughs of meanings of the popular and the people. But that perception is gained at the expense of a moral and cultural flatness. This one-dimensionality of cultural studies as to questions of moral or cultural value is undoubtedly embedded in the very definition of 'culture' which the discipline builds upon. Tony Bennett has made two linked points in his definition of culture. Firstly, 'culture consists of all those *practices* (or activities) that *signify*; that is, which produce and communicate meanings by the manipulation of signs in socially shared and conventionalized ways' (Bennett 1981: 79). Secondly, 'In the case of the rituals that comprise the domain of lived cultures . . . physical objects may take on a signifying value'. As examples of these physical objects that signify meanings and which may come to possess a signifying value, Bennett mentions Christmas presents and the meanings which surround the items of a 'traditional' Christmas dinner (Bennett 1981: 79). What is noticeable about both of these quotations, which are perhaps amongst the most basic building blocks of the cultural studies enterprise, is that they both deny the chance of the creation of any discourse about the moral or cultural value of activities or practices. *All* that can be discussed is signifying value; any notion of meanings beyond signification is pushed off the agenda of things which can possibly be said. Cultural studies is therefore a study of surfaces and the *attribution* of depths rather than a study of (actual or potential) hidden meanings.

Cultural studies is predicated on the notion that there is nothing ineluctible about culture. Now, I am not saying that there *is* something beyond words in culture, but it can be speculated (as an intellectual or even a spiritual possibility) that there *might* be. And it is perhaps worthwhile conducting an intellectual investigation of culture which does indeed make that wager on, and seeks to understand and explain, the possibility of the ability of some cultural products and practices to transcend the time and the place of their original emergence (for a far more elegant statement of this kind of position, see Steiner 1989). Only in that way can there be any sort of *meaningful and principled* critique of where we are in the here and now.

It is this fundamental vacuity and lack of seriousness of cultural studies as a moral and indeed cultural enterprise, which goes a considerable way towards explaining the increasingly obvious predictability of the discipline (the predictability mentioned at the beginning of this study. Indeed, it might also be this lack of seriousness which explains a great deal of the appeal of cultural studies. It does not *matter*; it is a more or less pleasant diversion from the problems of the world).

Instead of examining the pre-conditions of its own discourse, that is to say instead of carrying out a cultural study of cultural studies, the discipline has rather tended to become a more or less terminally circular and self-justifying narrative. Cultural studies is now only about some things and, increasingly, it is now only really associated with certain authorial names. The evidence which is used in one text tends to be derived from another text written within the narrative. There is no significant perception of the possibility of other ways of studying similar problems or, indeed, of the actual material existence in books of those other ways (for example, it is stunning that the Cultural Studies examination of sport and leisure pays so little attention to the work of Norbert Elias). The circularity and insularity of the discipline is to be understood as nothing other than a response to the fact that Cultural Studies has no coherent object of inquiry. It says it is about popular culture but, of course, popular culture is nothing. This difficulty is avoided by a desperate self-referentiality. In the lonely hour of the last instance, cultural studies is only helpful and useful because cultural studies says that it is.

It is only from a position outside of the narrative of cultural studies that all of these difficulties with the discipline come into the light. As Edgar Allan Poe realized in his story 'The Purloined Letter' there is a certain, 'moral inapprehension by which the intellect suffers to pass unnoticed those considerations which are too obtrusively and too palpably self-evident'. That inapprehension operates within the discipline but it need not prevail from a position outside of cultural studies. Indeed, once it is realized that cultural studies might well be structurally incapable of saying anything of moral or cultural importance about the media (or for that matter anything else), then perhaps the time has come to move into an alternative disciplinary field. Not because the alternative can be better or answer every question that it might be possible to ask, but simply because an alternative way of seeing might be able to pose and resolve different problems, and raise and nurture different doubts; that is, until the time has come for it too to have its preconceptions revealed.

For the time being then, any attempt to think around the questions of the impact of the media on moral and cultural values can, perhaps, best be carried out from a sociological perspective. That at least is one of the possibilities that this book will build upon and explore.

Chapter 2

The culture industry

I have argued that the difficulty with the constituted discipline of cultural studies is twofold. Firstly, instead of helping to explain the impact and ramifications of the media, actually the discipline simply repeats the claims of the media themselves that they are important. I suggested that this problem arose because cultural studies is a product of the social and the cultural world which is dominated by the media. As such, the media are the precondition for cultural studies; the discipline can only proceed if it takes the media for granted and does not actually turn its critical eye upon them. Indeed, in relation to the media, cultural studies does not *have* a critical eye. Secondly, cultural studies is a problematic discipline because it devastates any ability to talk in a meaningful way about the value of cultural goods or activities.

Certainly, cultural studies has wonderfully revealed many if not all of the conceits and arrogant, essentially political and class-based, assumptions behind the elevation of some things and not others to the status of 'proper' and 'official' culture (cultural studies does this through its analytic of hegemony), but all cultural studies has done is replace the now discredited claims of one constituency of 'the people' with a new and astonishingly flat, one-dimensional, world of value called popular culture. Within the world of cultural studies, this notion of popular culture is used to applaud the cultural activities and values of those social and cultural groups which are identified as currently dominated and which are therefore understood as the constituent parts of a new and a more democratic construction of hegemony. (Here then, it is simply assumed that a hegemonic bloc made up of 'the people', which is currently dominated as opposed to dominant, will necessarily be more acceptable politically and even morally. It will be, so to speak, doubly popular. To say the least, this is a fairly large assumption to make.)

Indeed, within the practice of the naming of activities and objects as popular culture, things which are taken to be unpleasant are not actually criticized or condemned so much as just ignored (witness the roaring silence that surrounds such things as the racism and of course the sexism of some working-class cultures). In other words, cultural studies has ended up looking rather like a simple inversion of the parent it wished to kill off. It has destabilized one series of power relations simply in order to put forward an alternative series of relations which seem to be more stable precisely because they are built on the ashes of the old structures. Cultural studies simply, and in some ways rather un-interestingly, challenges one construction of hegemony in order merely to replace it with another. But cultural studies stops at precisely this point when it might become pertinent and important to investigate some of the implications and preconditions of its own intellectual and prac-tical hegemony.

The result of these problems is that cultural studies as it is presently constituted and carried out can say little of critical importance about the media as shapers of cultural and moral values. If it is hoped to talk about these kinds of concerns, it is necessary to look elsewhere for inspiration. Undoubtedly one of the most helpful places to look is towards the work that was carried out by the German sociologist and cultural critic Theodor Adorno; the work he carried out on his own and in co-operation with his friend and colleague Max Horkheimer. Adorno and Horkheimer are two of the leading names associated with what has become known as the Frankfurt School. The School is commonly identified with a very European kind of social and cultural criticism which sought to bring together the insights of Karl Marx with the traditions of Kantian and Hegelian philosophy, the sociology of Max Weber and the psychoanalytic theories of Sigmund Freud. This work was first carried out in Germany in the years immediately before the Nazi take-over in 1933. After Hitler came to power, the members of the Frankfurt School went into exile. Adorno and Horkheimer eventually arrived in the United States.

Now, although both Adorno and Horkheimer are important in any attempt to understand the significance of the impact of the media on cultural and moral values, I will tend to pay a greater amount of attention to the work that Adorno rather than Horkheimer carried out on his own. As he grew older Adorno's analysis of the cultural significance of the media became a lot clearer both to himself and to his readers. Mean-while, after his work with Adorno, Max Horkheimer followed a rather different avenue of philosophical and sociological inquiry which was more concerned to explore the meanings and practices of reason and rationality than the media as such (although Horkheimer had already carried out an important study of culture in his essay 'Art and Mass Culture' which is included in Horkheimer 1972).

Two main themes run through the work Adorno did on his own and with Max Horkheimer. Firstly, the work is concerned to explain how it could possibly be that something as barbaric as Nazism could emerge in one of the centres of European culture. Secondly, the work Adorno and Horkheimer carried out whilst they were in exile was motivated by what amounted to a massive culture shock. Both Adorno and Horkheimer were highly cultured European men and yet they found themselves in a world they utterly failed to understand; the world of Hollywood and Mickey Mouse. Here, then, Adorno and Horkheimer were also concerned to try to work out quite why and how an entire nation could be so seduced by a picture of a mouse with big ears. Adorno and Horkheimer were concerned to try to understand the basis of the culture shock they experienced when they arrived in the United States. But at no time did they think that the sense of shock was in some way attributable to them and whatever shortcomings they might or might not have had; they were utterly confident that their failures to grasp the pleasures of Mickey Mouse were actually due to Mickey Mouse and everything that he could be taken to represent and suggest.

Yet Adorno and Horkheimer had reasons for their surprise, distaste and contempt. Their reaction to the American cultural scene was due to something more than a personal disregard for the world they found. They could justify their reactions to themselves and, moreover, to their readers. These reasons are embedded in a series of assumptions about the meaning and the significance of what culture *ought* to be about. It is these oughts which provide the basis for a most devastating critique of what culture is about thanks to the institutions and the arrangements of culture and especially the media in Western, capitalist, social relationships.

Perhaps the series of assumptions about what culture ought to be about are expressed most clearly in Adorno's solo work. In one of his essays Adorno made the following claim about culture. Here it is clear that, for him, culture is about all of those things that are different from, if not in opposition to, the demands and requirements of everyday life (and so at the very outset, Adorno's definition of culture serves to distance his work from the narratives of cultural studies. It is worth recalling Bennett for whom culture is basically day-to-day life. Adorno would have none of this). Adorno wrote that: 'Culture, in the true sense, did not simply accommodate itself to human beings; but it always simultaneously raised a protest against the petrified relations under which they lived, thereby honouring them' (Adorno 1991: 86). Adorno also proposed that there is a fundamental difference between culture and what he termed 'practical life' (Adorno 1991: 53) and that consequently, culture ought to be, and truly really is, critical of the static relationships of the day-to-day: 'Culture – as that which goes beyond the system of self-preservation of the species – involves an irrevocably critical impulse towards the status quo and all institutions thereof' (Adorno 1991: 100).

Basically, Adorno's claim is that culture ought to be something distinct from the 'petrified relations' of the 'status quo' of 'practical' and everyday life. Adorno sees daily life as something that is static and stuck. It is here today and, in fact, here again tomorrow and the next day and the next day. For Adorno, this everyday life is nothing other than a most terrible oppression of all that we can be. It traps us in routines and therefore stops us from doing new things. This is an understanding of the facts of daily life that is not too far removed from some of the comments Max Weber made towards the end of his classic analysis of *The Protestant Ethic and the Spirit of Capitalism*. In that book, Weber had traced the genealogy and the legacy of the movement of the Puritan concept of the calling from a religious asceticism to an economic-rational asceticism. As Weber says: 'when asceticism was carried out of the monastic cells into everyday life, and began to dominate worldly morality, it did its part in building the tremendous cosmos of the modern economic order' (Weber 1930: 181). But, Weber argues, this movement has tended only to mean that humanity has become trapped in the routines and the requirements of the everyday. For Weber, the domination of the Protestant Ethic means that humanity is a prisoner of the iron cage of what Adorno was later to call 'petrified relations'. Weber sees the history of the capitalist institutions and arrangements in terms of a journey towards spiritual death; for him there has been nothing other than, 'a departure from an age of full and beautiful humanity, which can no longer be repeated in the course of our cultural development than can the flower of the Athenian culture of antiquity' (Weber 1930: 181).

There are indeed significant similarities between the themes of Weber and Adorno (although the nostalgic vein is not so strong in Adorno as it is in Weber – Adorno more remorselessly believes that this world has become the only one we can have; for him, nostalgia would simply be a way of avoiding the horrors of our present). After all, for Adorno there is no doubt that everyday life is oppressive and repressive in such a way that we are all 'given to understand that what is most important is understanding the demands of "real life" and fitting oneself properly for the competitive realm' (Adorno 1991: 53). Speculation has been destroyed and demolished by the tyrannical domination of the dull compunctions of material reality.

So, for Adorno, culture ought to be a glimpse of other possibilities. According to his appreciation, culture ought to possess the ability to show us that there is more to life than things like learning transferable skills and becoming clerks. It ought to be *critical* and, in fact, it is nothing if it is *not* critical. Culture ought to inspire us to see how suffocating life is if all we want is to make our way in the world without ever asking why the world is like it is. Culture is consequently an enrichment and a challenge to everything that we are and might possibly be. It is a protest against the institutions that try to keep us in our place by giving us trivial rewards. Therefore, it is a true and proper honouring of humanity as opposed to all of the paper honours that are so important in daily life. For Adorno, culture involves no financial rewards or pay-back; and so, for him, it is yet all the more valuable. (It is obvious that already the terrain and presuppositions of the analysis of culture has moved into a wholly different intellectual world than that which is occupied by cultural studies.)

Once again, it is possible to detect traces of the ghost of Max Weber in Adorno's arguments. Weber too believed that the full potential of humanity was being hemmed in if not given a life sentence by the prisons of routine. As Weber wrote: 'Limitation to specialized work, with a renunciation of the Faustian universality of man which it involves, is a condition of any valuable work in the modern world; hence deeds and renunciation inevitably condition each other to-day' (Weber 1930: 180). Hence, the more we achieve in the material world (that is, the more we make and build; the more we produce through the requirements of rational capitalism; the more paper honours we are given), all the more are we fated to renounce the potential we might have in the world of the spirit. With this aspect of Weber's work, it is possible to see some of the seeds of the problem which Adorno and Horkheimer were later to make famous as the thesis of the *Dialectic of Enlightenment* (Adorno and Horkheimer 1972).

Weber is important because his approach to sociology, indeed his version of sociology, goes a significant way towards the opening up of a distinction between the ideals of the age (what ought to be) and the practices of the age (what is). It is exactly this kind of method which Adorno and Horkheimer were to use to great effect in their attempt to unravel the implications of the media on cultural and moral values. In other words, everything they say about what culture *ought* to be is in many ways only meaningful to the extent that this is precisely what culture no longer *is*. Each pole of this ought/is dichotomy validates, illustrates and adds force to the other. Adorno's recurring point (and the point that he developed with Max Horkheimer; see Adorno and Horkheimer 1972) is that, thanks in no small part to the activities and operation of the media, culture is no longer like it should be. Instead of standing in a critical relationship to everyday life, the media have made culture and especially the arts of music and painting a part of daily life. And so the media have played a not insignificant role in the destruction of all of the value of art. In the process the media have also managed to help transform the possibility of enlightenment into the probability of barbarism. This is the core of the analysis of the *culture industry*.

In an essay which he wrote towards the end of his life, Adorno located the time and the place of the emergence of the idea of the culture industry very precisely indeed. He wrote that 'The term culture industry was perhaps used for the first time in the book *Dialectic of Enlightenment*, which Horkheimer and I published in Amsterdam in 1947' (Adorno 1991: 85). The basic claim of the essay in the *Dialectic of Enlightenment* (which is chapter four of the book) is that the oppositional and the critical (and therefore what might be called the transcendental) dimensions of art have tended to be wholly destroyed. The culture industry has taken things like books, paintings and pieces of music and turned them into films, posters or records in order simply to make money or entertain the audience by helping them forget about their everyday problems. Consequently, books, paintings and pieces of music have, in fact, become integral parts of our daily lives. As such, the oppositional qualities and the inherent value of all of these cultural products has been undermined. Within the thesis of the culture industry, it is a more or less central argument that the media and cultural value actually tend to be somewhat incompatible.

According to Adorno and Horkheimer, the culture industry has done nothing other than destroy the value of art by pulling it into daily life. And by extension, therefore, the culture industry has destroyed the ability of art to celebrate and honour humanity. For Adorno and Horkheimer 'Movies and radio need no longer pretend to be art. The truth that they are just business is made into an ideology in order to justify the rubbish they deliberately produce' (Adorno and Horkheimer 1972: 121). Adorno and Horkheimer were in no doubt why so much of this 'rubbish' is produced: 'They call themselves industries; and when their directors' incomes are published, any doubt about the social utility of the finished products is removed' (Adorno and Horkheimer 1972: 121). So, the culture industry is not at all producing art when it releases films or broadcasts radio and television programmes. Quite the contrary, it is just doing in the cultural world much like a Henry Ford does in the world of transport.

It should be noted that Adorno and Horkheimer always refer to the culture *industry* in the singular as opposed to the culture *industries* in the plural. They do this because, for them, all of the branches of the media tend to operate as a uniform and a monolithic system. For Adorno and Horkheimer there is simply no significant difference between what the movies do to literature and what photographs in magazines do to paintings. They believe that it is misplaced and wrong to make any distinctions between different media forms and different media texts. They state that 'Films, radio and magazines make up a system which is uniform as a whole and in every part. Even the aesthetic activities of political opposites are one in their enthusiastic obedience to the rhythm of the iron system' (Adorno and Horkheimer 1972: 120). A few sentences later they comment that 'Under monopoly all mass culture is identical' (Adorno and Horkheimer 1972: 121). And, just to drive the point home a little more, they write that the implication and effect of the operation of this monolithic and monopolistic culture industry is 'no more than the achievement of standardization and mass production' (Adorno and Horkheimer 1972: 121).

Adorno and Horkheimer draw out the implications of all of this in a few passing comments about the cinema. Arguably, however, the comments can be applied to television as well. They suggest that 'Real life is becoming indistinguishable from the movies. The sound film . . . leaves no room for imagination or reflection on the part of the audience' (Adorno and Horkheimer 1972: 126). In other words, the cinema stunts and restricts the imaginative abilities which Adorno and Horkheimer say ought to be stimulated by art. And so whatever the cinema touches ceases to be art in the true and fullest meaning of the word. Instead, all of the dazzling technical effects of the cinema create so much noise and movement that our abilities to think are quite swamped. Indeed, Adorno and Horkheimer imply that the movies are popular precisely to the extent that they produce so much sound and fury that thought becomes impossible. The movies are valuable in the material terms of daily life since they hinder any speculation on their value as art or culture in themselves. Adorno and Horkheimer are prepared to admit that the movies might well be extremely entertaining, but they insist that if the movies are entertaining it is only because the audience has been virtually dehumanized and can now be palmed off with any rubbish. 'The stunting of the mass-media consumer's powers of imagination and spontaneity does not have to be traced back to any psychological mechanisms; he must ascribe the loss of those attributes to the objective nature of the products themselves' (Adorno and Horkheimer 1972: 126).

Adorno, for one, never felt a need to revise substantially this diagnosis and assessment of the effects of the media on art and cultural value. All that really changed was the clarity of his presentation. As he lived longer and seemed to see all of the pessimistic claims of the *Dialectic of Enlightenment* bear fruit, so he became able to spell out the meaning and effects of the culture industry all the more clearly. As such, in his essay which recalls the origins of the *Dialectic of Enlightenment* Adorno is able to provide a very succinct definition of what the term culture industry actually means. He writes of the culture industry: 'In all its branches, products which are tailored for consumption by masses, and which to a great extent determine the nature of that consumption, are manufactured more or less according to plan' (Adorno 1991: 85). In other words, the culture industry provides culture as it were from above and in accordance with its definitions of what the audience (which is redefined as the mass of consumers) wants. 'This is made possible by contemporary technical capabilities as well as by economic and administrative concentration' (Adorno 1991: 85). Moreover, within the rationale of the culture industry, 'The seriousness of high art is destroyed in speculation about its efficacy; the seriousness of the lower perishes with the civilizational constraints imposed on the rebellious resistance inherent within it as long as social control was not total' (Adorno 1991: 85).

When he makes this distinction between the 'seriousness of high art' and the rebelliousness of the 'lower', Adorno tends to sound remarkably like some of the theorists cultural studies has been most keen to attack. After all, Adorno is basically saying that high art is that which possesses the values of the transcendence of daily reality. High art is that which can inspire the contemplative and the speculative imagination of different worlds and different conceptions of the good life. Adorno seems to be assuming that the true value of high art is located precisely in its separateness. But the lower art is much more involved in daily life. Indeed, when Adorno talks about its rebelliousness, this comment only really makes sense if the rebellion is understood as a cultural response to the circumstances of material daily life. Lower art is thus a consequence of the here and now, whereas high art is something quite distinct from it and in fact transcendent of material reality. But Adorno's analysis is made quite subtle because he is prepared to see both high and lower art as serious in their own, admittedly different, ways. There is the hint that Adorno's reference to 'lower' is not entirely meant in an evaluative sense. He sees both high and low art as about something important and crucial; but this only makes the impact of the culture industry all the more tragic. For Adorno, the culture industry does not just reduce high art to the lower by asking only of its financial worth; it actually trivializes and makes cretinous absolutely all cultural activity and production.

Adorno's position can be thrown into especially sharp relief through an analysis of an essay he wrote on jazz. This essay is, perhaps, one of the most notorious pieces of cultural analysis ever carried out by an academic. It is invariably cited as the finest possible example of the inherent elitism of Theodor Adorno. It should be obvious that Adorno does rather lay himself open to this charge of elitism. There is no doubt that Adorno has few if any kind words to say about jazz. But the point which has to be made in Adorno's defence is that he is quite able to justify and defend his interpretation of the significance and awful, barbaric, implications of jazz. There is much more here than simple distaste; that is why the essay repays close scrutiny.

Adorno and Horkheimer took a few swipes at jazz in the *Dialectic of Enlightenment*, but the attitude towards this kind of music is expressed most clearly, and in a more developed form, in Adorno's essay 'Perennial Fashion – Jazz' (Adorno 1989). The main claim of the essay is very clear indeed. Basically, Theodor Adorno contends that with jazz it is possible to see an especially fine example of all of the terrible tendencies that are associated with the culture industry. Specifically, Adorno utterly rejects the perhaps common-sense and familiar view that jazz is a highly innovative kind of music which expresses the rebelliousness either of the musicians or of an oppressed social group. Adorno will have none of this, and, on the contrary, argues that jazz is in fact a thoroughly standardized kind of music which is churned out by the culture industry because it is profitable. For Adorno, the much announced rebelliousness and originality of jazz is just a stylistic trick developed by the culture industry in order to sell more product.

According to Adorno, the promises that surround jazz are entirely fraudulent. The audience only accepts these kinds of claims because they have been thoroughly duped over the years by the publicity machine of the culture industry. Adorno writes of jazz: 'everything unruly in it was from the beginning integrated into a strict scheme . . . its rebellious gestures are accompanied by the tendency to blind obeisance, much like the sado-masochistic type described by analytic psychology' (Adorno 1989: 200). Here, then, Adorno is saying that jazz music can no longer be innovatory, it can offer nothing new, because it operates according to the regulations of a strict standardization which is tied up with the demands and the requirements of the culture industry. Indeed, the rebelliousness of jazz has been restrained by the rational require-ments of conformity. Consequently, whenever jazz seems to be at its most revolutionary it is, in fact, at its most obedient. This is what Adorno means when he compares jazz to the 'sado-masochistic type described by analytic psychology'. He explains that this type 'chafes against the father figure while secretly admiring him' (Adorno 1989: 200). To explain further, with jazz:

> A helpless, powerless subject is presented, one that is ridiculous in his expressive impulses. Now the formula of jazz is this, that pre-cisely by virtue of his weakness and helplessness this subject repre-sented by irregular rhythms adapts himself to the regularity of the total process, and because he, so to speak, confesses his own impot-ence, he is accepted into the collective and rewarded by it. Jazz projects the schema of identification: in return for the individual erasing himself and acknowledging his own nullity, he can vicariously take part in the power and the glory of the collective to which he is bound by this spell.
>
> (Frankfurt Institute 1973: 113)

The conclusion is clear: 'While to the naive consciousness jazz, now long standardized, occasionally seems anarchic, the expression of un-inhibited erotic impulses, it permits these impulses only in order to cut them off and to reassert the system' (Frankfurt Institute 1973: 113).

As such, jazz has exactly the same cultural value and exactly the same ability to transform daily life and make us think again about everything we do as a coffee cup. As Adorno puts it with a suitable degree of disgust and outrage: 'What enthusiastically stunted innocence sees as the jungle is actually factory-made through and through, even when, on special occasions, spontaneity is publicized as a featured attraction' (Adorno 1989: 202).

Adorno believes that jazz is a product of the culture industry and that it can therefore have nothing original, challenging or truly exciting about it. Any appearances to the contrary are, in fact, mere deceptions. They are tricks. Indeed, 'the so-called improvisations are actually reduced to the more or less feeble rehashing of basic formulas in which the schema shines through at every moment. Even the improvisations conform largely to norms and recur constantly.' Adorno goes on to put the matter extremely succinctly: 'The range of the permissible in jazz is as narrowly circumscribed as in any particular cut of clothes' (Adorno 1989: 201). In other words, jazz is something that is made and bought off the peg. It has as much to do with the revolution, and with the imagination of different ways of life, as a bank clerk's suit: 'Jazz is taken for granted as an institution, house-broken and scrubbed behind the ears' (Adorno 1989: 206).

It is as if Adorno had been able to look ahead to see everything that would happen to pop and rock music. Of course, I am making a rather large jump in the argument here, but the point is that Adorno's ideas are not just exhibits in the museum of sociology or even cultural studies. Adorno's ideas and arguments are worth exploring precisely because they seem to be able to say so much about the present day. There can be little doubt that everything he says about jazz can be applied to other kinds of music as well. It is hard to think of any example of popular music which has not been subjected to the pressures towards standard-ization and conformity that the culture industry involves. Perhaps one of the clearest expressions of this process can be found in the records of The Clash. They started life as a very angry punk rock band who were going to free youth from the tyranny of having to listen to has-beens like Elton John and The Rolling Stones. They ended up pretending they were The Who with particularly short hair-cuts. (A similar story of the take-over of the initial rebelliousness of punk by the culture industry can be extracted from Savage 1991.)

Adorno's essay on jazz can be used to help develop an understanding and appreciation of what happened to The Clash in the late 1970s and early 1980s. Adorno's views inspire the hypothesis that what happened to The Clash is, in fact, symptomatic of all rebellion and innovation in a world where art is dominated by the culture industry. The Clash could do nothing other than end up looking like all the bands they so despised in their early days. And this transformation happened despite the fact that The Clash had so accurately spotted the tendencies which would eventually tame them. As Joe Strummer sang in the song '(White Man) in Hammersmith Palais' which was released in June 1978: 'You think it's funny, turning rebellion into money'. But to see exactly how rebel-lion was indeed turned into money, and how quickly the process can take hold it is only necessary to listen to the *The Clash* album of 1977 and then to *Sandinista!* of 1980. The one is innovation and raw energy to the other's air of going through the motions. Moreover, whereas the 1977 album is a very precise, tight and focused aggression, *Sandinista!*

rather slops around over six frequently self-indulgent sides. Exactly the same kind of story can be extracted from *This is Video Clash*; as the name implies, this is a tape of the videos which went with many of the band's singles. They start off as the rebellious voice from the streets and end up playing Shea Stadium. In the terms suggested by Adorno's theory of the culture industry, the fact that The Clash released a triple album would be proof of nothing other than the ability of the record company to get away with more things thanks to the effects on the audience of relentless advertising. The aggression ceased to be rebellion and instead it became an advertising slogan.

As to The Clash themselves, it rather seems as if they were in fact quite aware of the process that had given them success at the expense of their rebelliousness. By the time *Sandinista!* was recorded, the band was trying to say something about the impact of the culture industry. But the reflections on the old days of freedom were little more than impotent nostalgia. All the band could do was recall the days of 1977 and 1978 when records were made 'Without even the slightest hope of a 1,000 sales' (a line from the song, 'Hitsville U.K.'). But the point was, of course, that those days had long since gone and now The Clash was forced to live in the world of the culture industry; the world of 'slimy deals with smarmy eels' ('Hitsville U.K.' again).

Consequently, it can be suggested that The Clash were forced to produce a totally standardized form of music if they wanted to be certain of a 1,000 sales or more. Any experimentation could only be allowed if the record company permitted it, or if the wool could be pulled over the record company's eyes for long enough. To this extent then, the story of The Clash can be taken as a very good illustration of what might happen to music as soon as it has been taken up by the culture industry. Certainly, a band can become much more popular; advertising and multi-media releases can make sure of that. But the music itself is forced into a straitjacket from which little or no escape is possible. After all, and as Adorno put the matter himself, 'The investments made in "name bands," . . . and, even more important, the money used to promote musical bestseller programs like "The Hit Parade" by firms who buy radio advertising time, make every divergence a risk' (Adorno 1989: 202). But if the producers of the music are trapped like this, then the situation is not much better from the point of view of the consumers: 'They are expected to want only that to which they have become accustomed and to become enraged whenever their expectations are disappointed and fulfilment, which they regard as the customer's in-alienable right, is denied' (Adorno 1989: 202).

In all of these ways then, the history of punk can easily be read as a tale of the destruction of everything punk could and should have been. The history indeed tells a tale of the movement from rebellion to money. Of course, these comments represent an application of Adorno's point of view to events about which he could know and therefore write absolutely nothing. But it does seem to be relatively easy to use the insights contained in the essay on jazz to explain a phenomenon like punk even though it is, on the face of the matter, many worlds away from what Adorno would have wanted to talk about.

It is clear from examples such as his views on jazz quite why Theodor Adorno is not too popular within the circle of the discipline called cultural studies. Certainly, his reputation amongst the practitioners of cultural studies is not helped by his tendency to make claims of the order that: 'Anyone who allows the growing respectability of mass culture to seduce him into equating a popular song with modern art because of a few false notes squeaked by a clarinet . . . has already capitulated to barbarism' (Adorno 1989: 205).

Consequently, Adorno's impact on the cultural studies' study of the media has been rather less positive than the impact of his some-time colleague, Walter Benjamin (for details of the relationship between Benjamin and Adorno, see Buck-Morss 1977). Now, what is interesting is how Walter Benjamin had a perspective on the cultural significance and impact of the media which is to a considerable extent the exact opposite of Adorno's. For Adorno, of course, everything is rather terrible, but Walter Benjamin was far more inclined to see some good coming out of the ability of the culture industry to reproduce and sell things like books, music and, in particular, paintings. Benjamin expresses his views most clearly in his famous essay on 'The Work of Art in the Age of Mechanical Reproduction' (Benjamin 1973). If it is crass but nevertheless slightly true to say that Theodor Adorno was tending towards a cultural elitism, then in 'The Work of Art' essay, Walter Benjamin reveals himself to be rather more prone to lean towards a cultural democracy.

Of course, from Adorno's point of view, if any work of art is reproduced then it is made a part of everyday life and it loses its status of being something different and apart. In other words, according to Adorno a work of art is unique but the products of the culture industry are standardized and open to reproduction again and again. This quality of uniqueness is what Adorno called the *aura* of the work of art. The aura is something that surrounds the original. But the aura tends to be destroyed by reproduction. For Adorno this is a very bad thing indeed because it means that art loses its value of being different.

But according to Walter Benjamin, the tendency towards the destruction of aura is actually a very good thing. This is because the
beauties and the attractions of art are taken out of the galleries and the
concert halls and given a wider circulation; they are made more accessible as the fake mystery which has come to surround them tends to be
eaten away. For Walter Benjamin the tendency towards the destruction
of the aura means that anyone anywhere has access to art on exactly the
same basis as anyone else. In other words, the interpretation of art is
made available to all and art is, therefore, democratized. According to
Benjamin, all of this can happen because it is now possible technically
to reproduce art. Photography can reproduce paintings so that I can look
at the *Mona Lisa* without having to go to Paris, and sound recording can
reproduce concerts I never attended (and need never attend again). So
for Benjamin the work of art becomes part of my everyday life and I can
use it in any way I want, irrespective of what the 'experts' might say,
and quite without having to do difficult and expensive things like visit
art galleries or concert halls. Thanks to technology, then, culture has
been given to the people at large and has been taken away from the
self-proclaimed self-established elite groups. This is because the aura of
authenticity has been attacked and challenged. 'From a photographic
negative, for example, one can make any number of prints; to ask for the
"authentic" print makes no sense' (Benjamin 1973: 218). As Walter
Benjamin goes on to put the matter: 'the instant the criterion of authenticity ceases to be applicable to artistic production, the total function of
art is reversed. Instead of being based on ritual, it begins to be based on
another practice – politics' (Benjamin 1973: 218).

In itself, this comment might not have been too far removed from
what Adorno was trying to say. However, the key difference is that
Adorno would mean something quite contrary to Benjamin by the word
'politics'. The kind of politics of culture that Adorno seems to advocate
is a largely contemplative and speculative meditation of the possibility
of alternative ways of being and alternative orders of things. For
Adorno, culture ought to be the occasion of us thinking differently (for
Adorno's development of his 'political' position and his response to
those who argue that his stress on thinking means quietism, see the essay
entitled 'Resignation' in Adorno 1991). Benjamin's politics is a much
more solid activity in the material world of daily life. This connection to
material political processes has two aspects in Benjamin's work. Firstly,
Benjamin seems to posit some kind of historical identity between events
in the history of culture and events in the history of the class struggle.
As such, 'With the advent of the first truly revolutionary means of

reproduction, photography, simultaneously with the rise of socialism, art sensed the approaching crisis which has become evident a century later' (Benjamin 1973: 218). Secondly, Benjamin, quite unlike Adorno, believes that the ability to reproduce art means that now art can become an enriching and vital part of the daily lives of the workers. Indeed, the workers can become art experts for themselves, and thus, this aspect of culture is released from the rituals of the professionals. Moving from photography to the movies, Benjamin proposes that: 'It is inherent in the technique of the film . . . that everybody who witnesses its accomplishments is somewhat of an expert'. Indeed, instead of sensing ourselves to be prisoners of the world we can instead begin to see ourselves as active participants in a world of our own making: 'the newsreel offers everyone the opportunity to rise from passer-by to movie extra' (Benjamin 1973: 225).

In Walter Benjamin's argument, all of this means that thanks to the media (and especially thanks to the technologies of the reproduction of images), culture becomes something that is enjoyable precisely because it does not require the kind of deep and devoted concentration so important to the argument of Adorno. Benjamin implies that, thanks to the media, culture has been given back to the busy and the permanently distracted inhabitants of the modern world. As Benjamin expresses the matter: 'A man who concentrates before a work of art is absorbed by it. He enters into this work of art the way legend tells of the Chinese painter when he viewed his finished painting' (Benjamin 1973: 232). Max Weber and Theodor Adorno would almost certainly have wanted to defend this response to art; in losing ourselves in the painting we are able to escape the oppressive rationalities of daily life, enter into different arrangements and, thus, return to this world with a more critical eye.

But Benjamin feels that the media make another kind of response possible, a response which does not involve a (however temporary) loss of our selves: 'In contrast the distracted man absorbs the work of art' (Benjamin 1973: 232). Here, Benjamin is saying that when we go to a work of art or cultural production we are invariably seeking a distraction from the exertions of daily life; culture is a tool for our re-creation. Art provides this distraction and, indeed, enters into our daily lives precisely because we are able to bring it into ourselves; precisely because we are able to absorb it without ever losing sight of the problems of the material world (whereas, of course, in Adorno's scheme, 'real life' problems are indeed transformed during the moment of concentration on the cultural product).

Benjamin thought that these processes were at their clearest in the reception of film. Through the example of film he is also able to pull together his comments on the effect of reproduction on the aura of art and its surrounding rituals. Benjamin writes that 'The film makes the cult value recede into the background not only by putting the public in the position of critic, but also by the fact that at the movies this position requires no attention' (Benjamin 1973: 233–4). Consequently, 'The public is an examiner, but an absent-minded one' (Benjamin 1973: 234).

Benjamin's views are expressed, developed and used very clearly by John Berger in his book *Ways of Seeing* (Berger 1972). In the book, Berger tries to explain the impact of photographs on the ways in which art is approached and understood. He is, of course, especially concerned to explore the nature of the relationship between the originals and what Benjamin would have called the 'mechanical reproductions'. Berger too wants to democratize art, but he is aware that the technological possibilities of photographs are often subverted by how the photographs are used as texts in newspaper and magazine advertisements (an important consideration which Benjamin overlooked). According to Berger, 'Because works of art are reproducible, they can, theoretically, be used by anybody'. But there is a gap between the theory and the practice. After all, Berger tells us, 'Yet mostly – in art books, magazines, films or within gilt frames in living-rooms – reproductions are still used to bolster the illusion . . . that art makes inequality seem noble and hierarchies seem thrilling' (Berger 1972: 29).

However, Berger believes that the gap can be overcome by us as individuals. He points out that most of us have a noticeboard of some kind on which we pin pictures and other odds and ends. According to Berger, when we do this we are using the reproductions of art for our own ends, and according to our own designs; and so we are revolutionizing it by making it a part of our daily lives. We are practising a 'total approach to art which attempts to relate it to every aspect of experience' as opposed to 'the esoteric approach of a few specialized experts who are the clerks of the nostalgia of a ruling class in decline' (Berger 1972: 32). He carries on in a way that betrays profound (but acknowledged) debts to Benjamin's as opposed to Adorno's discussion of the fate of the aura of the original work of art. As John Berger puts it, the technological ability to reproduce art means that 'For the first time ever, images of art have become ephemeral, ubiquitous, insubstantial, available, valueless, free'. Adorno would of course agree with all of that, and he might not even disagree with the conclusion Berger draws from his observation. Berger says that works of art 'have entered the mainstream of life over which they no longer, in themselves, have power' (Berger 1972: 32). The difference is that Berger, following Benjamin, rather tends to applaud this process, whereas Adorno is quite outraged by it. The similar stories have very different stories to tell about the fate of cultural values.

For Adorno, the fact that we might be happy to pin a postcard of the *Mona Lisa* to our wall only goes to show what the culture industry has done to us. It has reduced us to such a level that we are happy to be fobbed off with cheap copies; we feel absolutely no need to see the original because we think that it has nothing to say to us. And, in any case, we all know that only elitists go to art galleries. For Adorno, we would not be taking art out of the hands of the experts and revolutionizing its appeal when we put a reproduction on our wall. Quite the contrary, we would just be sticking up a more or less pretty piece of paper. And if we are happy with that, well, according to Adorno, then we are just barbarians.

When he refers to barbarism, Adorno is making a point that goes much further than cheap insults. For Adorno, the word barbarism is a way of throwing into relief all of the implications of the culture industry and, by extension, all of the implications of the thesis of the *Dialectic of Enlightenment*. In their book, Adorno and Horkheimer draw on the definition of enlightenment which was given in 1784 by Immanuel Kant. In an essay of that year in which he attempted to answer the question, 'What is Enlightenment?', Kant had written that, '*Enlightenment is man's emergence from his self-incurred immaturity. . . . Immaturity* is the inability to use one's own understanding without the guidance of another' (Kant 1970: 54; original emphasis. Kant is discussed in Adorno and Horkheimer 1972: 81–6.) In these terms, something can be identified as barbaric to the extent that it represents and involves a restriction of the ability of the individual to think for him- or herself; barbarism is telling people what to think or do. Barbarism is a return to immaturity. As such, fascism is barbaric in a triple sense; it is barbaric culturally, morally and also of course physically. But the culture industry is also barbaric in a cultural and a moral sense. This is because it too prevents thought; because it too consigns man to wallow in immaturity and thus denies the chance of enlightenment.

If enlightenment means making sense of the world for oneself, without a belief in ghosts in the machine, then the operation of the culture industry means that a belief in such ghosts increases. Adorno justified this kind of desolate and dark analysis of the impact of the culture industry on enlightenment when he carried out an especially brilliant analysis of the astrology column of the *Los Angeles Times* (Adorno

1974). He argues that newspaper astrology columns can be taken to represent an indication of what has happened to the high hopes of culture in the process of enlightenment. Adorno wants to explore how astrology is one example of a wider tendency whereby we have been rendered immature; we do not think for ourselves and even less do the products of the culture industry help us to think. Instead, they just offer us ridiculous superstitions. What this means is that people tend to, 'take astrology for granted, much like psychiatry, symphony concerts or political parties; they accept it because it *exists*, without much reflection, provided only that their own psychological demands somehow correspond to the offer' (Adorno 1974: 15). After all, and as if to emphasize the culture industry's tendency towards immaturity, 'the mechanics of the astrological system are never divulged and the readers are presented only with the alleged results of astrological reasoning in which the reader does not actively participate' (Adorno 1974: 15). All of this is important to Adorno because he understands the popularity of astrology columns to be 'a "symptom" of some tendencies of our society as well as of typical psychological trends among those this society embraces' (Adorno 1974: 81).

Adorno argues that astrology represents a kind of barbarism because it indicates not just a decline of the sense of the importance and autonomy of the individual but also a decline of the independence of social institutions and arrangements themselves. Astrology is a means by which the individual is able to come to terms with a world which she or he feels to be exactly the kind of iron cage that Max Weber spoke about.

Firstly, Adorno says that there is no longer any aspect of the life of the individual which remains outside of the institutions and processes of rational societal organization: 'The intermediary processes between social control and the individual tend to vanish and the individual has once again to obey the direct verdict of the groups at the helm of society' (Adorno 1974: 82). Astrology is a reflection of, and a response to, this situation 'For, while people recognize their dependence and often enough venture the opinion that they are mere pawns, it is extremely difficult for them to face this dependence unmitigated' (Adorno 1974: 82). Astrology is that mitigation; it is a way in which I can excuse my dependence since it is written in the stars (I can tell myself that it is not my fault; there is nothing I can do).

Secondly, Adorno emphasizes the significance to the appeal of astrology of the sense that we are caught in a world which is heading towards self-destruction irrespective of what we might do (Adorno sees the tendencies towards self-destruction in nuclear weapons; our equivalent is global warming). Astrology helps us come to terms with the anxieties about self-destruction. It 'gives some vague and diffused comfort by making the senseless appear as though it had some hidden and grandiose sense'. But, meanwhile, astrology confirms 'that this sense can neither be sought in the realm of the human nor can be properly grasped by humans' (Adorno 1974: 84). This is more or less precisely the immaturity Kant railed against at the end of the eighteenth century.

Thirdly, astrology is the faith of what Adorno calls a 'supposedly sceptical, disillusioned people.' Simply, 'The cult of God has been replaced by the cult of facts, just as the fatal entities of astrology, the stars, are themselves viewed as facts, things, ruled by mechanical laws' (Adorno 1974: 84).

But this still leaves the problem of why astrology is so popular. Certainly, Adorno is able to explain that astrology is tantamount to barbarism, but so far he has not explained why a paper like the *Los Angeles Times* was prepared to publish an astrology column. His answer to this problem is, perhaps, somewhat predictable. Here, Adorno quite explicitly returns the argument to the frame of the analysis of the culture industry. Astrology is given such space in the *Los Angeles Times* precisely because it appeals to a certain kind of person (the kind of individual who senses the world as a prison) and, therefore, precisely because it is a way of selling newspapers. 'In view of this commercial success, astrology is taken up by more powerful economic agencies which take it away from the crystal-gazer atmosphere . . . (just as the big studios took away the movies from the amusement park booths)'. These power houses of the culture industry take up astrology and 'make it "respectable" and thus utilize it commercially on a large scale' (Adorno 1974: 88). And so, instead of enlightening us, the culture industry simply deceives us (the formula of this sentence is obviously an allusion to the title of the chapter on the culture industry in the Dialectic of *Enlightenment*).

Basically, Adorno is suggesting that astrology represents and reflects a world that individuals can no longer understand or make for themselves. Astrology is the consolation prize for those whom Max Weber called the 'specialists without spirit' and the 'sensualists without heart' (Weber 1930: 182). The culture industry cashes in on this sensibility. Adorno himself sees the fans of astrology as people who, basically, have been rendered cretinous by the intellectual division of labour in modern social arrangements. It is worth quoting Adorno at some length on this point. His tendency to talk with a mixture of contempt and compassion for those who are seduced by the empty products of the media becomes quite clear:

While the naive persons who take more or less for granted what happens hardly ask the questions astrology pretends to answer and while really educated and intellectually fully developed persons would look through the fallacy of astrology, it is an ideal stimulus for those who have started to reflect, who are dissatisfied with the veneer of mere existence and who are looking for a 'key,' but who are at the same time incapable of the sustained intellectual effort required by theoretical insight and also lack the critical training without which it would be utterly futile to attempt to understand what is happening.

(Adorno 1974: 87–8)

Perhaps this kind of comment does mean that Adorno's work is open to the charge of elitism. But it is too easy to level that charge against him and, moreover, it is actually to miss the point of what he is trying to say. Yes, Adorno does say that astrology (just like jazz) is barbaric and he does have no good words to say about these kinds of popular cultural forms and texts. But the whole point is that he does not therefore despise the ordinary viewers and listeners (although, admittedly, he is not too fond of the pleasures of the astrology and the jazz fans). Rather, he despises the system which produces all of this rubbish and the critics who try to convince people that what they get from the culture industry is actually worth having. In other words, the evident elitism of Theodor Adorno has to be read as part of a profound and serious attempt to recover humanity from the idiot distractions of squeaked saxophones and astrology.

Of course, writers like Benjamin and Berger also applaud and try to recover humanity. They try to do this by demystifying art and by showing how the technologies of reproduction tend to destroy aura and therefore democratize access to paintings, music and the like. As such, they tend to see the culture industry and the media in an immensely positive light precisely because they can take culture out of the hands of the experts. Their argument is not against the culture industry as such, but rather against the culture industry as it is presently organized. For the likes of Benjamin and Berger it is vitally important to recognize and to defend the ways in which ordinary people use reproductions of art in their daily lives.

But from the point of view of someone who is following Adorno, that kind of celebration of popular culture is too easy. It merely involves a celebration of what happens as opposed to indicating what *ought* to happen. Put another way, from Adorno's point of view, Benjamin and Berger are guilty of being overfamiliar with existing social and cultural arrangements. As such, they are unable to carry out any kind of critique of them. All they do is describe the uses of the media and say that it must be a good thing that the media are popular and available for use by different people in different ways. But that would be exactly what the captains of the culture industry would also say. So, perhaps there is nothing very radical at all about the identification of the potentially radical uses of the existing media.

But, for Adorno, there would be a yet more profound problem with the claim that the technologies of the reproduction of images have a radical potential. It is clear from the drift of Benjamin's and Berger's essays that they think it is extremely important that photography is able to produce an image which is more or less the exact replica of reality. But all this means for Adorno is that, firstly, the crucial distinction between art and reality is once again destroyed and that, secondly, art itself becomes little more than a great big museum. Art becomes a dead thing to be plundered for images as opposed to a living challenge to the everyday. And, somewhat un-surprisingly, this process logically implies, if not actually means, the spiritual death of humanity: 'If mass culture has already become one great exhibition, then everyone who stumbles into it feels as lonely as a stranger on an exhibition site' (Adorno 1991: 71).

What Adorno is trying to do, of course, is defamiliarize the familiar. He is concerned to carry out a fully sociological investigation of the media. That is perhaps another of the reasons why he has nothing good to say about them. For Adorno, to say that the media and the culture industry are wonderful and democratic institutions would simply be to cosset people in their preconceptions. What he is trying to do is show his readers that the world can actually be a very different place than it is at the moment. In order to show that, he must therefore force his readers to actually think about what the culture industry is doing, what it actually means to prefer jazz over Beethoven or astrology over responsibility for one's own life. Adorno is trying to carry out a rhetorical strategy of defamiliarization in his essays on the culture industry.

With this rather grand sounding reference to a 'rhetorical strategy of defamiliarization' I am making a relatively straightforward point. The word 'defamiliarization' of course refers to the purpose and intention of the use of a sociological imagination. Meanwhile, something can be called rhetorical when it uses deliberately chosen phrases or words to communicate the thrust of an argument with an increased force. Rhetoric is often very showy and punchy, so that the claim the writer is trying to make comes across to the reader all the more powerfully. So, when I say that Adorno's essays like the one on jazz rely on a 'rhetorical strategy of defamiliarization', I am simply saying that he uses deliberate overstatement to make his points seem a lot more powerful than they otherwise might be. He tends to use showy phrases so that the reader is *forced* to think about the impact of the media on their own lives.

Indeed, in the introduction to the *Dialectic of Enlightenment* Adorno and Horkheimer explicitly made the point that the style of their writing, its mode of address, itself represents a little something by way of an attempt to free humanity and thought from the clutches of the culture industry. Since the culture industry provides standard products which are frequently applauded for their clarity and ability to be understood by anyone, so Adorno and Horkheimer argue that any writing that seeks to challenge this reign of the clear must be a little unclear. Only in that way is it possible to defamiliarize the thought processes and ways of life that the culture industry permits.

According to Adorno and Horkheimer, the acceptance of the notion of clarity, the acceptance of the prevailing definitions of things, and the acceptance of what happens, actually causes us to fall into a serious trap. After all, 'Since that notion declares any negative treatment of the facts or of the dominant forms of thought to be obscurantist formalism or – preferably – alien, and therefore taboo, it condemns the spirit to increasing darkness' (Adorno and Horkheimer 1972: xiv). With his dismissals of and disdain for things like jazz and astrology, Adorno is, then, struggling to enlighten the human spirit. This means that the more difficult his work is to read the more he succeeds, precisely because we have to think very very hard about exactly what it is that Adorno is actually trying to say. For Adorno, it is important that any discussion of the culture industry, and therefore of the media, is neither entertaining nor, for that matter, a repetition of how the culture industry defines itself.

As an example of this, it is worth looking at the reasons for Adorno's refusal to talk about something called the 'mass media'. Adorno's rejection of this phrase is based on the belief that it is too harmless and that it therefore obscures the true nature of the media. The phrase implies that the media are in the business of serving a mass they are concerned about. In other words, the phrase mass media implies that the mass is the subject towards which media activity is directed. Adorno says that this is a deception, a myth and plain wrong: 'The customer is not king . . . not its subject but its object' (Adorno 1991: 85). He continues with more difficult language. He makes the point that to talk in terms of the phrase 'the mass media' implies a concern with the masses which the media actually do not have: 'Neither is it a question of primary concern for the masses, nor of the techniques of communication as such, but of the spirit which sufflates them, their master's voice' (Adorno 1991: 85–6). According to Adorno, then, the phrase mass media is misplaced because it implies that the masses are getting what they want. But for him, the masses are just getting what it is decided to give them. The phrase culture industry is Adorno's attempt to open up a way of explaining all of this.

Moreover, Adorno consequently becomes able to explain why he is so dismissive of the cultural forms of the masses and the media which, by their own declarations, serve them. He explains that the responsibility for the contempt is actually not his. After all, 'If the masses have been unjustly reviled from above as masses, the culture industry is not among the least responsible for making them into masses and then despising them' (Adorno 1991: 92). So, Adorno's contempt is indeed driven, at least in part, by a rhetorical concern. He is so dismissive and outraged by cultural and media activities like jazz and astrology precisely because the culture industry which propagates these forms is itself dismissive of the consumers it claims to serve. Adorno is so dismissive of us precisely so that we think about *why* he so dislikes what we do; precisely so that we can see that whatever we might think about Theodor Adorno, the fault is not just his.

In the work and the integrity of Theodor Adorno it is possible to see an example of intellectual courage of the highest possible order. Adorno opens himself up to the most vitriolic criticism and yet he is prepared to accept it and encourage still more. After all, Adorno seems to be saying, if you hate what I say about you, you might start thinking about *why* I say all of these things. It is for precisely this reason that Adorno's essays can be regarded as some of the most important contributions to the study of the media and the fate of moral and cultural values that have ever been provided. Certainly, Adorno's prose is not easy (but he did not want it to be; if we want easy things we can watch the television), and his answers are difficult to accept. He offers no happy endings (because, for Adorno, if we want happy endings we can go to the movies). But if Adorno's essays are read in the spirit he intended, then he does make us think for ourselves. He certainly makes it difficult to take the media entirely for granted.

Chapter 3

The audience

It was one of my main arguments in the last chapter that Theodor Adorno (with Max Horkheimer, of course) offers an understanding of the culture industry which is amongst the most profound and stimulating accounts of exactly what it is that the media mean and imply for moral and especially cultural values. According to Adorno, in the last instance the media mean nothing other than the barbarization of humanity and of the value of art, literature and nearly everything else that ought to be important. The pleasures the media offer thus amount to little more than so many stupidities. Indeed, from a point of view indebted to Adorno it would almost certainly tend to be argued that any study of the products involved in, or inspired by, the media would simply be a repetition and an added twist to that process of barbarization. From an 'Adornoesque' perspective it is at the very best quite trivial and at the worst a further assault on the possibility of a meaningful enlightenment to defend the popular cultural forms of day-to-day life. In the terms outlined by Adorno, the narratives of cultural studies would almost certainly be identified and criticized as involving little more than a tightening of the dehumanizing grip and idiot distractions of the culture industry.

In the light of the work of Adorno (and of course Horkheimer) it is not too unreasonable to claim that the media make us cultural cretins, utterly unable to make any sensible discriminations of value. For Adorno, the culture industry means that we become unable to imagine that there might be a significant qualitative difference between the original of the *Mona Lisa* and the postcard we stick on the wall. The culture industry also means that we no longer have to come face to face with our responsibility in the world; instead we make excuses through the use of astrology columns. In this chapter, the focus of attention is going to change a little. In the discussion of Adorno and Horkheimer, a number of hints were made about what it is like to be a member of the

audience of the culture industry. This chapter will explore the nature of
the audience in a little more detail. The best place to start is with a very
simple point: in the work of Adorno and Horkheimer it is quite clear that
some relationship of cause and effect, of action and response, is assumed
to exist between the media and their audiences. In other words, it is
simply taken for granted that media forms are essentially involved in the
relationships, practices and the procedures of a *dialogue*.

I have taken this reference to dialogues from the work of Mikhail
Bakhtin and his colleagues who were active in the Soviet Union in the
1920s and early 1930s. The technical meaning of the reference to
dialogues is spelt out with reasonable clarity by V.N. Voloshinov in his
article on 'The Construction of the Utterance' (Voloshinov 1988). In the
article, Voloshinov is trying to understand and analyse the social nature
of speech. By way of providing a definition of the meaning of the term
dialogue, Voloshinov makes the comment that, 'We usually respond to
any utterance made by our interlocutor, if not with words, then at least
with a gesture, a movement of the hand, a smile or by shaking the head,
etc.' (Voloshinov 1988: 117).

Now I want to suggest that the media texts which the individual picks
up or turns on must be understood in precisely this way of the dialogue.
The media are involved in relationships of a dialogue because they
inspire some kind of response on the part of the reader, viewer or
listener. Media texts are fundamentally *dialogic* (that is, they are
fundamentally involved in a dialogue). This is because they are intended
to provoke some kind of response from the audience. To this extent, it is
even possible to understand a dialogic media text as something similar
to an academic lecture. After all, 'any utterance, public speech, lecture,
etc. is intended for a listener, i.e. to be *understood* and *responded to* by
him. (Of course, not directly – you cannot interrupt a public speech or a
lecturer with your response)' (Voloshinov 1988: 118). Voloshinov goes
on to make it quite clear that something like a lecture can only be fully
explained and fully understood if attention is directed towards the
audience(s) who seek to make sense of, and respond to, the text they are
receiving: 'The utterance looks for his *agreement* or *disagreement*, in
other words for a *critical reception* on the part of the listener ("the
audience")' (Voloshinov 1988: 118).

One of the big debates which can be seen to run through the literature is
about the exact balance of power within this dialogic relationship. Certainly, it can be seen that it is vitally important to pay attention to the media
audiences. But this does not begin to approach a resolution of the problem
of whether the audiences really are partners in a more or less equal dialogue

or whether, on the contrary, they have been turned into little more than passive dupes who will accept anything that is thrown out to them (perhaps this way of outlining the problem shows that the concern with hegemony which runs through the cultural studies work of Tony Bennett and Stuart Hall is also intelligible as an analysis of dialogues). In other words, the key cultural debate can be seen to revolve around the possibility that the media dialogue has, in fact, been transformed into something that is rather more by way of a monologue. And in a monologue, of course, one person speaks to the exclusion of all others; the audiences do not respond, they just soak up what they are given.

Theodor Adorno and Max Horkheimer provide one especially profound and thoroughly worked out expression of this possibility that the media dialogue is really a monologue on the part of the culture industry. They do this by thinking through, and reflecting on, some of the implications of their analysis of the culture industry. In their discussion of the audience, which is stated most clearly in a couple of the brief notes which can be found at the back of the *Dialectic of Enlightenment*, Adorno and Horkheimer make three main points. Firstly, they argue that the culture industry sees and makes a single audience. Here, the argument seems to be that since the culture industry itself is a monolith, then the audience of the culture industry will be monolithic also. Secondly, they suggest that this single monolithic audience of the culture industry is a passive mass; it is not active in and for itself. Thirdly, Adorno and Horkheimer argue that within the single, mass audience each individual is isolated from every other individual. As Adorno and Horkheimer say, 'Modern communications media have an isolating effect; this is not a mere intellectual paradox' (Adorno and Horkheimer 1972: 221).

It is worth thinking about this comment by Adorno and Horkheimer. On the one hand they are saying that the media turn us all into isolated individuals. But on the other hand, they are saying that the media do this more or less equally to everyone. The paradox which Adorno and Horkheimer highlight has two component parts. Firstly, it means that we experience the media alone. Secondly, it means that the media treat us as if we were all the same. Bringing these two parts together, the conclusion of Adorno and Horkheimer is that the media therefore have the effect of levelling down all individuals, so that, from the point of view of the culture industry, they actually do become the same in all important respects. The media challenge anything that stands out as different. From the point of view of the media, all social and cultural differences, all of the specific relationships and activities which make us precisely who we are, become things to be marginalized in the interest of the construction and maintenance of a passive and a conformist audience.

Adorno and Horkheimer argue that these processes of the levelling down of the audience can be seen especially clearly with the case of the adulation of film stars. Adorno and Horkheimer write that, 'The cult of celebrities (film stars) has a built-in social mechanism to level down everyone who stands out in any way' (Adorno and Horkheimer 1972: 236). The media tell us, for example, that film stars are beautiful or particularly skilful in their relationships with the opposite sex. They are examples for us to follow, and if we do not follow the example set by film stars, well, we are either ugly or disastrous sexual performers. We are all reduced to the level of the extent to which we are like one actor or another. And, according to Adorno and Horkheimer, the media tell us that we really ought to do something about ourselves if we are incapable of being like the characters we see on the screen (and so we conform to the demands of the culture industry either by avidly reading self-improvement manuals and film-star biographies in order to get tips on success, or we conform by making the excuses permitted by astrology columns). In other words, the media treat us as members of a mass, and it forces us to do and look like what we think everyone else does and looks like. However, Adorno and Horkheimer do identify a nagging doubt and emptiness at the heart of all this imitation and levelling down. They say that we look up to celebrities because 'Part of their moral influence consists precisely in the fact that they are powerless in themselves but deputize for all the other powerless individuals, and embody the fullness of power for them' (Adorno and Horkheimer 1972: 236). We are weak in face of the culture industry; consequently, we idolize film stars all the more since they appear to be so strong. (But, of course, the stars are victims of the culture industry also. Perhaps this dialectic can be taken to be the basis of much of the continuing appeal of the mythic symbol of Marilyn Monroe; Monroe is at one and the same time a role model and a victim just like us. The symbolism of Marilyn Monroe basically says: conform, do not dare to stand out. These aspects of the myth of Marilyn Monroe are quite clearly expressed in Summers 1985.)

The paradox highlighted by Adorno and Horkheimer is, then, that the media assume and operate in terms of a *mass* audience of *individuals*. According to the analysis of Adorno and Horkheimer, the media give everybody the same programmes irrespective of their social and cultural position. The media treat everybody as basically the same and, therefore, as a simple and single mass. But, and here is the paradox, the technologies of communication, and indeed some of the media texts, have the effect of isolating each individual from every other individual.

Adorno and Horkheimer explain that 'The lying words of the radio announcer become firmly imprinted on the brain and prevent men from speaking to each other; the advertising slogans for Pepsi-Cola sound out above the collapse of continents' (Adorno and Horkheimer 1972: 221).

Adorno and Horkheimer are suggesting that, thanks to radio (and, it should be added, thanks to television), we have forgotten how to speak to each other. Moreover, and, in any case, the announcers tell us that we would not wish to speak to our neighbours if we knew the real truth about what goes on behind the lace curtains. But Adorno and Horkheimer are also making the much larger point that even though the map of the world can change, even though empires can crumble and fall apart, all we can hear is the jingle of soft drink advertisements. It might even be said that advertising has meant that political transformations have ceased to be about freedom, emancipation or all of the other great aims which have been the heritage of radicals since the French Revolution. Instead, it would rather seem to be the case that political transformations and enterprises are now rather more about nothing other than the struggle of some groups to secure the right to buy and consume junk food. Arguably, this change in the intentions behind political activity was demonstrated very clearly indeed during and immediately after the collapse of really existing socialism in Central and Eastern Europe in 1989. It would seem to be perfectly reasonable to suggest that what the people of, say, Czechoslovakia or East Germany were after was not the moral or political good life. They were just after hamburgers (see Lash 1990).

But, if Adorno and Horkheimer are to be believed, the impact of the media on the audience goes much further than the transformation of politics into pop music. They suggest that the media have turned the mass audience into a collection of isolated individuals and have thereby played a part in unravelling the moral bonds which link us all together. For Adorno and Horkheimer, the media have devastated the ties of social and moral solidarity. After all, 'the example of movie stars encourages young children to experiment with sex and later leads to broken marriages. Progress literally keeps men apart' (Adorno and Horkheimer 1972: 221).

According to Adorno and Horkheimer, then, the audience is important not because of what it does but because of what has happened to it. For them, the audience is important precisely because of the dehumanizing processes which have been unleashed and played out upon it. Their analysis works on the assumption that the individuals who make up the media audience should be active in their own right. Certainly, within the theory of art which runs through Adorno's understanding of the culture industry, the audience *ought to be* a partner in a dialogue. Indeed, Adorno's position is that truly valuable art and cultural production requires and promotes this dialogue. But, thanks to the culture industry, there is now a huge gap between what *ought to be* and what *is*. Instead of a dialogue, the media are involved in nothing other than a monologue which keeps the individuals in the audience isolated from one another irrespective of whether they are an audience in the cinema (where individuals sit next to each other) or in the sitting room (where individuals are often alone). So the point that Adorno and Horkheimer are trying to make is not that the media isolate individuals within the mass in a physical sense (although certain media technologies can do just that), but rather that the media isolate individuals from one another in a moral and a social sense. The media create an audience that cannot answer back.

Now, if it is permissible for the moment to return to Voloshinov to help explain what Adorno and Horkheimer are trying to say, it becomes possible to argue that the monologic form of the culture industry has undesirable consequences. It does not just mean that we have sex-crazed youth walking the streets of the cities. Somewhat ironically, it also means that the media become incapable of actually achieving their aims. This is another aspect of the paradox of the audience which Adorno and Horkheimer perhaps did not manage to grasp. The paradox is contained within their work but it always seems to slip away at precisely the moment when it should become glaringly evident. Essentially, the problem is that if Adorno and Horkheimer's diagnosis of the effects of the culture industry is correct, then it is actually impossible for the audience to be and repeatedly become the dupes of the media as they claim.

Imagine that you are a member of the kind of audience that is conjured up by Adorno and Horkheimer. You are sitting in front of the television, you are thinking about nothing apart from what is on the screen and you are utterly incapable of responding to what you see and hear. You are like this because, if Adorno and Horkheimer are to be believed, you are isolated from everyone else, and you have had all your hopes, ambitions and desires pushed out of you. All you hope for is a good day tomorrow according to the stars. As such, you do not participate in a dialogue with the television; rather it delivers a monologue to you. Now, imagine that an advertisement appears telling you that you will have a far better time in bed if you read a certain newspaper. Adorno and Horkheimer would argue that once you have seen this advertisement you will go out and buy the paper in order to educate yourself in the ways of sexual technique (but of course this technique

will not be an expression of individuality or even of individual tender-
ness and love; it will simply be a series of more or less mechanical and
rational tricks on the way to a better and bigger orgasm. Consequently,
sexual activity and passion become conformist too). However, that
action on your part means that the advertisement has been able to
establish a dialogue between you and it. But this is exactly what Adorno
and Horkheimer say cannot happen. If they are indeed implying that the
culture industry operates as a monologic form, then, by definition,
neither advertisements nor moral education through the media can
actually work. Voloshinov made this kind of point quite clear when he
said that 'The speaker who hears only his *own* voice or the professor
who sees only his *own* notes is no good at his job'. This is because 'He
weakens the force of his utterances, breaks the dialogic bond with his
audience and so devalues his talk' (Voloshinov 1988: 118).

The theory of the culture industry does indeed assume that all the
media hear are their own voices (and in these terms cultural studies
would be one source of the culture industry talking back at itself). After
all, the theory suggests that any other voices have been quite snuffed
out. But, and as Voloshinov makes quite clear, this kind of monologue
is quite unable to capture the attention of the intended audience and,
therefore, the message of complete conformism cannot get across.
Certainly, absolutely no practical response to the message is possible.
Any response (such as going to a shop to buy the newspaper and then
doing all of the things you are told to do) presupposes the kind of
dialogue which the very activity of the culture industry makes
impossible. In other words, the theory of the culture industry seems to
have a very fundamental logical flaw at its heart.

It might well be the case that this is a largely inevitable problem with
any sociological study of culture which argues that the media have
created a passive audience which is, however, trapped within the world
of consumer goodies and rationalized pleasures. Whether or not this
makes the problem a little more understandable is, of course, a totally
different matter. It is quite noticeable that the problem is also contained
in Richard Hoggart's book *The Uses of Literacy*.

At a first glance, the pretty massive jump from the subtle theoretical
arguments of Adorno and Horkheimer to the accessible nostalgia of
Hoggart's book might seem a little questionable. But it is not. They all
share a common belief that the media have created a passive, mass
audience which is nevertheless open to persuasion by advertising. In
other words, despite the otherwise very great differences between them,
Adorno and Horkheimer on the one hand and Richard Hoggart on the

other do rather seem to·be arguing about much the same things. They all want to try to understand what the media have done to social and cultural activity amongst the viewers and listeners. They all want to explain how it is that the media have 'unbent the springs of action' as Hoggart has nicely put it (Hoggart 1958). Adorno and Horkheimer develop their interpretation through theory, theorizing and cultural critique. Hoggart develops his interpretation by telling a tale about the fate of working-class culture in northern England (for the purposes of this book, it is not important whether Hoggart's book should be seen as a memoir, as cultural critique or as a piece of fiction; I leave it to you to work out the status of *The Uses of Literacy*).

Hoggart's book was written in the 1950s and, in Britain at least, it has become one of the founding texts of cultural studies. This is because Hoggart tried to understand what had been happening to the life and culture of the working class. He did this by concentrating on what he said the working class read and thought rather than on what they did and spent their money on (the kinds of questions about *material* life and relationships that largely motivated and shaped George Orwell's investigations in *The Road to Wigan Pier*). In so doing, Hoggart opened up the *culture* of working-class life to academic study.

But, Hoggart argued, the traditional working-class world was rapidly disappearing. Whereas the academic orthodoxy would have been concerned to show how the old order of working-class life was disappearing because of economic pressures, Hoggart said that it was disappearing because of changes in reading material. He gives economic or employment questions a very marginal place in his study. Hoggart is more concerned with 'changes in working-class culture during the last thirty or forty years, in particular as they are being encouraged by mass publications' (Hoggart 1958: ix). In other words, despite whatever shortcomings the book might have, *The Uses of Literacy* is indeed a truly cultural study.

Of course, Adorno for one was in little doubt that the products of the culture industry like jazz music and astrology had led to the cretinization of the listeners and readers. In many ways, Hoggart seems to suggest that mass publications have done much the same to his traditional working class. The difference is, that whereas Adorno says this with a mixture of contempt and disgust, Hoggart says it with a more resigned pity. Hoggart comments that the products of the media 'tend towards a view of the world in which progress is conceived as a seeking material possessions, equality as a moral levelling, and freedom as the ground for endless irresponsible pleasure' (Hoggart 1958: 282). This largely moral critique of the impact of the media is extended into what might be termed an educational critique. Here, Hoggart begins to sound a little like Adorno when he writes that, 'These productions belong to a vicarious, spectators' world; they offer nothing which can really grip the brain or heart' (Hoggart 1958: 282).

The similarities between Hoggart's views on the nature of the media audience and the views of Adorno and Horkheimer go even further. Hoggart also makes the point that within the mass audience all individuals are levelled down to a kind of common denominator. Hoggart makes this double-sided process quite clear when he writes that, thanks to the media, the members of his traditional working class are 'being presented continually with encouragements towards an unconscious uniformity' (Hoggart 1958: 283). He goes on to explain why these encouragements are accepted and how they lead to a mass audience of uniform individuals. Hoggart says that this media-propagated uniformity 'has not yet been found hollow by most people because it is expressed most commonly as an invitation to share in a kind of palliness, even though in a huge and centralized palliness' (Hoggart 1958: 283).

So far then, Richard Hoggart has been developing the idea that the audience is a mass of individuals. This is very much like Adorno and Horkheimer. But it is also noticeable that Hoggart and Adorno and Horkheimer would give slightly different reasons for why people are prepared to become isolated individuals within the mass audience. For Adorno and Horkheimer it is because all of the rebelliousness of individuals has been utterly crushed and diverted by the culture industry so that there is nothing left except passivity. As such, Adorno and Horkheimer's audience is indeed a group of virtual dunces (but, it must be stressed, they are dunces because of what has happened to them rather than because of their own lack of abilities). Meanwhile, Hoggart argues that his 'working-people' accept all of the processes to which they are subjected because they are dazzled by the glittering prizes offered in advertisements. These advertisements pretend to give to 'working-people' everything they have always wanted: freedom, equality, progress and a sense of community. But, in fact, all they get from advertisements is a destruction of their traditional ways of activity and a fake 'palliness' (it is worth thinking about not just the emotive and very northern resonance of Hoggart's use of the word 'palliness' but also its fundamentally masculine connotation).

It is at this point that Hoggart ends up getting as stuck as Adorno and Horkheimer on the paradox of the difference between the dialogic and monologic media texts. Just like the two representatives of the Frankfurt

School, Hoggart ends up concluding that his audience is turned into a mass of individuals because it responds to (that is, enters into a dialogue with) the monologue of media texts. Hoggart too says that the media make 'working-people' passive, but he too utterly fails to notice that the audience can only be made passive if it responds to the media in a passive way. Or in other words, the media are only monologic because they are in fact dialogic.

This paradox of the dialogic nature of the monologic is especially obvious with Hoggart. He brings the pieces of the paradox together for us whereas we had to draw the paradox out of Adorno and Horkheimer. On the one hand, Richard Hoggart is in little doubt about how the audience reacts to, and therefore enters into a dialogue with, media claims of freedom and community. He says that 'Most people will respond to such an appeal the more readily because it seems to have much in common with some older working-class attitudes' (Hoggart 1958: 283). But, on the other hand, Hoggart is equally convinced that 'The result is a high degree of passive acceptance, an acceptance often only apparent and often qualified at present, but which is a ground for more dangerous extensions' (Hoggart 1958: 283). It is extremely hard to know how both of these comments can be true at one and the same time.

In all, then, it seems to be reasonable to suggest that despite initial appearances and for that matter despite its reputation, Richard Hoggart's book is actually of very little help in developing an understanding and an interpretation of the media audience. He too, horribly and seriously comes quite unstuck on the paradox of the dialogue and the monologue. Not to put too fine a point on the matter, in the last instance his book does not actually hold together as a coherent argument. But perhaps Adorno and Horkheimer are not much better. They too cannot square the circle that activity is required of the audience if the audience is actually to be passive. The audience has to be able to respond to media texts in a way that denies the possibility of a response (the trickiness of that sentence is part of the point I am trying to make).

Yet there is a greater problem with Adorno and Horkheimer. Basically, it is that their understanding can *interpret and explain* the nature of the audience but it is generally incapable of generating any kind of a *description* of what it is like to be a member of the audience. When all is said and done, it is rather difficult to put oneself into the picture Adorno and Horkheimer paint (even though they paint it so very well). To explain something is to give meaning or an interpretation; to explain is to be able to account for something and to state reasons for why it happens. But to describe something is to tell what it is like; to describe something is tantamount to painting a picture of it in words. It is this painting which the work of Adorno and Horkheimer quite fails to do.

Perhaps recent work within the narrative of cultural studies can help to overcome this difficulty. Within the narrative and the discipline a lot of attention has been directed at exactly this question of describing what it is like to be a member of the audience (this is of course yet another manifestation of the central cultural studies concern to understand where 'the people are at'). And it is also quite clear that much of this material seems to cast doubt on the validity of the broad theoretical sweep of the kinds of comments which can be associated with Theodor Adorno and Max Horkheimer. As such, it is useful and important to look in a little detail at some of this cultural studies material on the audience. This material is largely derived from *empirical investigation*. It should be clear that Adorno and Horkheimer reach their conclusion from the construction of social and cultural theories. Their work contains very few references to what individuals actually do, and the observations which can be found in places like the *Dialectic of Enlightenment* are pretty broad to say the least. In many ways, this kind of tendency to explain everything everywhere in a paragraph is typical of some of the more theoretical versions of sociology and especially the sociology of culture. But a lot of the work in cultural studies is more concerned to describe the precise and the prosaic detail of daily life. It is therefore far more specific and it is built upon extremely careful research into what individuals actually do and think (or at least, what individuals *say* they do and think). This is what might be called an *empirical* method; it is based on observation rather than theory.

Something of a middle point between the theoretical and the empirical approaches to the audience can be found in John Fiske's book *Television Culture*. Fiske's main concern is to explain how audiences watch television and, indeed, how they derive pleasure from their activities. This means that he is more or less exclusively concerned with the meanings that surround a media text. These meanings revolve around the question of the relationship between the ideological dimensions of the media texts and how they are reworked and challenged (resisted) by their audiences. The classic definition of the meaning of ideology is to be found in the work of Karl Marx and Frederick Engels. They proposed that, 'The ideas of the class which is the ruling *material* force of society, is at the same time its ruling *intellectual* force' (Marx and Engels 1970: 64). Marx and Engels are saying that the groups and classes that own and control the means of production will be better able to communicate their views than other groups or classes. Any competing views will be silenced, co-opted or destroyed. Fiske is concerned to explain and explore how and to what effect ideology can be seen to be represented in television culture.

Fiske draws a very important distinction between television *programmes* and television *texts*. He points out that 'A program is a clearly defined and labeled fragment of television's output. . . . We know that an ad is not part of a program, we know when one program finishes and another starts'. Fiske, therefore, defines television programmes as, 'stable, fixed entities, produced and sold as commodities, and organized by schedulers into distribution packages. *Dallas* is the same program whether it is broadcast in the USA, North Africa, or Australia' (Fiske 1987: 14). When he understands the television programme in this way it seems as if Fiske is going to start exploring the relationships that turn the television programme into a commodity which is made and sold, bought and transmitted. But, for Fiske, these industrial, commercial and economic questions are of rather less interest than the cultural activities of watching on the part of the audience which tries to understand the programme. This series of viewings and interpretations by the audience turns the programme into a text. After all, 'Programs are produced, distributed, and defined by the industry: texts are the product of their readers' (Fiske 1987: 14). Fiske explains: 'So a program becomes a text at the moment of reading, that is, when its interaction with one of its many audiences activates some of the meanings/pleasures that it is capable of provoking' (Fiske 1987: 14). Consequently, 'one program can stimulate the production of many texts according to the social conditions of its reception. *Dallas* is a different text in the USA, in North Africa, and in Australia'. Fiske continues: 'indeed, it is many different texts in the USA alone' (Fiske 1987: 14). This is a thoroughly dialogic understanding of the media.

It is at this point that Fiske makes it clear that, for him, television texts are to be understood in terms of the question of ideology. Fiske builds his analysis on the hypothesis that 'Texts are the site of conflict between their forces of production and modes of reception. . . . A text is the site of struggles for meaning that reproduce the conflicts of interest between the producers and consumers of the cultural commodity' (Fiske 1987: 14). Basically, Fiske's argument is that the programme is produced by the culture industry and that it is structured around a limited range of meanings which are supportive of existing relationships of power and domination (that is, existing relationships of hegemony). However, the programme is read as a text by an audience which projects its own meanings and interpretations onto it. Inevitably, the series of meanings that the audience gets out of the text is derived from its position in the relationships of domination. This in turn means that there will be many different audiences for any given programme; each audience will have its own reading of the television text. Consequently, the interests of the programme makers to produce a bounded and clearly identifiable commodity tend to be subverted by the audiences, which actively create the meanings of the text for themselves. And each audience will construct the meanings of the text differently from other audiences because of its peculiar social and cultural position. (I think it is worth noting, however, that Fiske is a little vague about explaining whether pre-existing audiences read texts, or whether the reading of texts creates audiences. The question which Fiske seems to fudge a little is whether the audience creates the meanings or whether through being shared the meanings create the audience.) This diversity of interpretations is called *polysemy*.

According to Klaus Bruhn Jensen, polysemy may be defined as involving 'The argument . . . that several interpretations coexist as potentials in any one text, and may be actualized or decoded differently by different audiences, depending on their interpretive conventions and cultural backgrounds'. Jensen continues 'It is polysemy which may, in part, account for the popularity of the same media text with different audiences' (Jensen 1992: 219). In these terms, a popular media text is one that can be interpreted by a diversity of audiences for their own ends. But for John Fiske there is of course much more to polysemy than the popularity or otherwise of different texts among different groups of viewers. He sees the matter in political terms and writes that 'The structure of the text typically tries to limit its meanings to ones that promote the dominant ideology, but the polysemy sets up forces that oppose this control' (Fiske 1987: 93). The conclusion is clear: 'The hegemony of the text is never total, but always has to struggle to impose itself against the diversity of meanings that the diversity of readers will produce' (Fiske 1987: 93). (In this passage, Fiske is using the word 'hegemony' in a fairly straightforward sense where it means leadership or dominance.)

Fiske uses the idea that television texts are essentially dialogic to reveal a paradox at the very heart of television culture. He contends that the success of television 'in the financial economy depends upon its ability to serve and promote the diverse and often oppositional interests of its audience' (Fiske 1987: 326). The financial success of television culture, therefore, can only be guaranteed to the extent that matters of the communication of the ideology of the dominant social groups are thrown open to doubt. What the financial economy gives, the cultural economy of the everyday reading of television texts takes away (Fiske 1987: 316). In the everyday acts of interpretation which the television audiences carry out, Fiske sees a 'power to construct meanings, pleasures, and social identities that *differ* from those proposed by the structures of domination' (Fiske 1987: 317).

Even though Fiske's work is in itself quite persuasive, it is undermined by a fatal methodological weakness. Fiske's work confuses the possibility that the audience *might* carry out oppositional readings of media texts with the claim that therefore they actually *do* carry out such readings. Fiske is guilty of confusing a claim about what *could* happen with another claim about what *does* happen. Actually, a reading of Fiske's book *Television Culture* shows that there is absolutely no evidence whatsoever to back up his contention that television 'is the prime site where the dominant have to recognize the insecurity of their power, and where they have to encourage cultural difference with all the threat to their own position that this implies' (Fiske 1987: 326). Fiske merely asserts this point.

Fiske is guilty of arguing that because something *can* happen it therefore *does* happen. But there is actually no necessary connection between statements of what might be and what is. For example, it *might be* the case that I have got cancer but that statement (which is in itself quite true; I *might* have cancer) does not at all therefore mean that I *have* got cancer. Similarly, although it might well be the case that media audiences can carry out oppositional readings of media texts, that does not at all in itself prove or justify the contention that they do carry out such readings.

However, and notwithstanding this difficulty in Fiske's work, a difficulty which no doubt derives from his desire to find politics in the places of pleasure, his work is worth looking at because, perhaps unlike Adorno and Horkheimer, he does try so very hard to put the audience in the main frame of the analysis. For Fiske, the audience is an active agent which most certainly participates in relationships of a dialogue with media texts. Indeed, Fiske would have us believe that without such a dialogue of reading, the programmes broadcast by television would have little or no meaning. They would most certainly have a very minor cultural significance. Consequently, Fiske is primarily concerned to explain how it is that the activities of audiences are essentially extremely meaningful and meaning-giving to groups of individuals.

The nature of the difference between his understanding of the audience and the kind of understanding which can be found in the work of Adorno and Horkheimer has been summed up rather nicely by David Tetzlaff. As Tetzlaff says, 'Adorno and Horkheimer argue that the culture industry molds subjectivity with mechanical standardization . . . while John Fiske argues that ideological unification inevitably fails as different subcultural audiences create their own meanings from pop culture texts' (Tetzlaff 1992: 49). Unlike Adorno and Horkheimer, then, Fiske tries to develop an awareness of the subtleties and the different forms of dialogue within the responses and readings of the audiences. For Fiske it is simply too general, if not completely wrong, to suggest that all individuals within the media audiences are standardized and levelled down to some common denominator. Fiske rejects notions of monolithic audiences or monolithic readings. Instead, Fiske argues that the important thing to look at is how viewers actively and purposefully respond to the programmes and turn them into texts with meanings. And that implies that a great deal of attention should be paid to the conditions and contexts in which viewers engage in the practical and day-to-day activity of watching television.

Fiske is making a call for research that will enable a description of the processes through which media texts are made into meaningful parts of our everyday lives. Fiske wants to know exact details about the nature, significance and influence of the reading environments of the audiences. Fiske wants descriptions of the precise practices and pro-cesses which his explanation of television culture tells him take place. Indeed, he feels that such descriptions are potentially able to do much more than simply help with the understanding of how television is watched. He seems to think that descriptions can help explain the meanings of culture in general. After all, Fiske contends, 'The study of culture must not be confined to the readings of texts, for the conditions of a text's reception necessarily become part of the meanings and pleasures it offers the viewer' (Fiske 1987: 72). Basically, what Fiske is doing is making a call for ethnographies of the media audiences.

Ethnography is a well-known (although relatively recent) addition to the methods available to the social and cultural researcher. It has its origins in anthropology. In a useful introductory guide to this research methodology, David Fetterman writes that 'Ethnography is the art and science of describing a group or culture. The description may be of a small tribal group in some exotic land or a classroom in middle-class suburbia' (Fetterman 1989: 11). The description might even be of media audiences as they watch the television. Fetterman continues to explain that the ethnographer 'interviews relevant people, reviews records, weighs the credibility of one person's opinions against another's, looks for ties to special interests and organizations, and writes the story for a concerned public as well as for professional colleagues' (Fetterman 1989: 11).

All of this interviewing, recording and weighing tends to be concerned with attempts to unravel and describe the basic, taken-for-granted and rather predictable fabrics of our daily lives. It is no surprise, therefore, that media researchers should have some fondness for ethnographic methods. After all, in the terms outlined by Fetterman, it promises to be able to get to the very heart of the matter of the conditions that influence the ways in which audiences read texts. In its own terms at least, ethnography promises to be able to unlock the secrets of watching television.

Some of the first ethnographic work in the field of research into media audiences was carried out by Dorothy Hobson. She interviewed and observed women at home with their young children. Hobson wanted to try to understand the significance and the place of radio and television in the daily lives of these women. Through the use of interviews and observations, Hobson came to the conclusion that the broadcast media are extremely important in the daily routines of young women with children. Even though these women rarely tend to listen to the radio or watch the television very closely, and even though, therefore, the media are little more than the providers of background noise, Hobson says that for the women these media are 'important means of negotiating or managing the tensions caused by the isolation in their lives' (Hobson 1980: 109). Or, put another way, through her use of an ethnographic methodology, Dorothy Hobson was able to conclude that women who are stuck indoors all day with young children tend to turn on the television or the radio because it offers an escape from loneliness and boredom. These media offer a kind of company. For Hobson's young mothers, radio and television offer the possibility of the dialogue that is otherwise impossible for them; there tend to be few if any face-to-face partners with whom the young mothers might enter into a dialogue, and so they listen to the radio and television instead. Of course, whether or not that promise of a dialogue with the media is actually taken up by the women is another matter entirely.

But Hobson found that the women used the radio and television in another way as well. They used it to help organize the activities of their days. As Hobson puts the matter: 'the time boundaries provided by radio are important in the women's own division of their time' (Hobson 1980: 105). In other words, the women tended to use the media in such a way that they could divide the day into different time slots on the grounds of the kind of statement that if this is *Neighbours* it must be lunchtime. Here then, it is possible to go a little way towards describing exactly how it is that the media can become quite fundamental and taken-for-granted parts of our daily lives. They are the key time-markers in and of day-to-day routines. The media help us to know what we should be doing now.

Tania Modleski has extended these ethnographic insights and used them to research the specific question of the role and significance of soap opera in the daily lives of women. She believes that the chores of the housewife are repetitive but often interrupted by such demands as having to pay attention to other members of the family. The kinds of soap opera shown during daytime television help housewives to operate in this world of routine and interruption. Soap opera manages to distract women from housework because it operates on the basis of 'the very principle of interruptibility crucial to the proper functioning of women in the home' (Modleski 1984: 100). But perhaps just as importantly, soap opera manages to reinforce the ideological position of the house-wife as the carer of the whole family, who must be aware of the concerns of everyone without unduly identifying herself with the demands of anyone in particular. According to Modleski, soap opera tell a story about the lives of a number of individuals at the same time; the viewer is asked to be aware of the competing interests of each. The viewer knows more about the characters than the characters know about them-selves. As such Modleski says that the woman who watches daytime soap opera is 'a person who possesses greater wisdom than all her children, whose sympathy is large enough to encompass the conflicting claims of her family . . . and who has no demands or claims of her own' (Modleski 1984: 92).

However, it is perhaps with the name of David Morley that the ethnographic study of media audiences is now most often associated. It cannot be denied that Morley's book *Family Television* is both a clear example of what ethnography can do and a significant development of this particular research tradition (Morley 1986). The book is based on in-depth interviews with eighteen families who lived in south London in the spring of 1985. Morley describes the social and cultural position of this group of families: 'All consisted of households with two adults living together with two or more dependent children, up to the age of eighteen' (Morley 1986: 52). Now, it should be clear to even the most methodologically illiterate person that Morley's sample can hardly be seen as a representative cross-section of British society. Morley was extremely aware of this problem with the group he was researching but explained it away on the grounds of 'budgetary limitation' (Morley 1986: 52). But, in any case, perhaps the validity of Morley's findings are in many ways less important than the method he adopted to get them and the kinds of questions he asked his eighteen families.

Morley's intention was deceptively simple. He makes the rather good point that 'We all "watch television", but with how much attention and what degrees of commitment and response, in relation to which types of programming, in which scheduling spots?' (Morley 1986: 50). What Morley is doing is taking a very taken-for-granted claim (the claim that we all watch television) and then using ethnographic methods to show that it is actually far from self-evident precisely what it means to watch television. Different people watch television in different ways at different times of the day. Morley himself puts the same point a little more prosaically: '"Watching television" cannot be assumed to be a one-dimensional activity which has equivalent meaning or significance at all times for all who perform it' (Morley 1986: 15). Morley tried to illustrate and describe the nature of these differences by concentrating in particular on the different ways in which men and women indulge in the activity of 'watching television'.

Morley's work recalls some of the points made by Dorothy Hobson and Tania Modleski. He rightly points out that even though both men and women obviously watch television at home (that is to say, in the domestic sphere), nevertheless, the meanings of 'home' are rather different for each gender. For men, the domestic sphere is defined as a place of leisure and rest from work, whereas for women the domestic sphere is defined more as a place of housework. Consequently, men see themselves as able to watch television attentively (because they have nothing else to do at home), whereas women's viewing tends to be rather more fragmented (because they do have other things to do in the home).

Morley makes the distinction between how men and women watch television very clear indeed. He says of his sample that 'the men state a clear preference for viewing attentively, in silence, without interruption "in order not to miss anything"' (Morley 1986: 150). For the men, then, watching television is in many ways an activity that is kept separate from the interaction and relationships of family life. But Morley's women see the matter very differently indeed. For them, watching television is 'a fundamentally social activity, involving ongoing conversation, and usually the performance of at least one other domestic activity (ironing, etc.) at the same time'. Morley continues: 'Indeed, many of the women feel that to just watch television without doing anything else at the same time would be an indefensible waste of time, given their sense of their domestic obligations' (Morley 1986: 150). But Morley discovered that amongst his eighteen families, gender differences went much further than just *how* television was watched. There were also gender differences about *what* was watched. Morley writes that when he started to ask about people's programme preferences the 'respondents displayed a notable consistency . . . whereby masculinity was primarily identified with a strong preference for "factual" programmes (news, current affairs, documentaries) and femininity identified with a preference for fictional programmes' (Morley 1986: 162).

Stuart Hall is in no doubt as to the lesson that the reader should take away from this ethnographic information. Hall believes that Morley has finally and once and for all managed to shatter any notion that the media audience is a monolith. Hall states that thanks to Morley's research it can now be seen that 'We are not "viewers" with a single identity, a monolithic set of preferences and repetitive habits of viewing, all exposed to a single channel and type of "influence" and therefore behaving in predictably uniform ways'. Instead, Hall says (and here he begins to sound not unlike John Fiske), 'We are all, in our heads, several different audiences at once, and can be constituted as such by different programmes' (Hall 1986: 10).

Stuart Hall is not alone in his high estimation of David Morley's ethnography. Fred Inglis calls the work 'warmly entertaining' (Inglis 1990: 153). John Fiske, perhaps rather inevitably, draws a comforting political moral from Morley's tales of life by the gas fire. Fiske chimes in with a couple of claims along the lines that Morley has rescued the oppositional reader from the clutches of monolithic theorizing. On the one hand, thanks to the kind of ethnography that is illustrated most clearly in the work of Morley, 'Television, with its already politicized pictures of the world, enters a context that is formed by, and subjected to, similar political lines of power and resistances' (Fiske 1987: 77). Meanwhile, and on the other hand, it is now clear for John Fiske that 'The fears of the pessimistic Marxism that characterizes . . . the Frankfurt School [i.e. that characterizes Adorno and Horkheimer] . . . are contradicted by this culturalist and ethnographic approach to the understanding of television' (Fiske 1987: 93).

But it is possible to criticize Morley's ethnography. Firstly, Morley falls into his own version of the logical trap that ensnared John Fiske. Whereas John Fiske conflated statements of what might be with statements of what is, David Morley tends to conflate statements made by respondents about what they *think* they do with statements about what they *really* do. He misses the possibility that what we *think we do* and what we *really do* might actually be two rather different things. This methodological problem could have been avoided if instead of just interviewing his eighteen families, Morley had conducted sustained non-participant observation of their watching habits and practices (that is, if he had seen for himself whether there was a coincidence between what people said and what they did). Secondly, Morley's work has exactly the opposite problem to that which can be seen in the work of Adorno and Horkheimer. If it can be said that Adorno and Horkheimer *explain but do not describe*, then it can be said with equal validity that Morley *describes but does not explain*. When all is said and done, Morley tells us absolutely nothing that we do not know already. Morley does little or nothing to defamiliarize the everyday. On the contrary, all he does is simply write books about it. Certainly, work like that associated with Morley is fairly interesting in itself but, sociologically speaking, it is rather trivial.

This second difficulty is perhaps due to an inherent tendency of any ethnographic methodology. For want of a better phrase, this tendency can be called the *problem of the fetishization of everyday life*. Obviously this phrase and its meaning require some detailed explanation.

I am using the word 'fetishization' in much the same sense as Karl Marx used it in *Capital*. Marx explained what he meant by fetishization when he tried to work out why it is that commodities have such a hold and a fascination over the individuals who live in capitalist relationships of production (Marx 1938: 43). Marx explained that commodities are like this because we forget about the social relationships that made the commodity (such as the car or the television set or whatever) what it is. For example, a television set is fetishized when I talk about its wonderful sound reproduction but forget that it might well have been made by poorly paid slum-dwellers from the Third World. In these terms, then, advertising and the cultural analysis of advertising is a fetish because it blinds us to the conditions in which the commodities were made. If the advertisers are to be believed, all that is important to me is the diamond ring I give my fiancée; I do not need to worry about the human and environmental degradation that made it possible for the diamond to be mined in the first place.

In a nutshell, something is fetishized when it is seen independently of its social and cultural position and conditions of existence. The kind of ethnography that Morley carries out falls into exactly this trap of fetishization. Certainly, Morley is able to describe in very great detail all that his families say about what it means to watch television. But, importantly, in Morley's work these families are just dropped onto the page.

Apart from a couple of rather crude and simplistic references to the social class of each of the eighteen families, it is largely impossible to get any sense of their social and cultural positions. For example, Morley shows that his research sample watch television, but he is utterly incapable of explaining why they have a television in the first place. Similarly, he is utterly unable to say why his respondents think the television is important enough to devote so much time to watching it. Neither is he able to say in any way exactly why watching television should be an object of scholarly concern (perhaps his only justification would be to repeat the assertion that television deserves investigation because it 'is where the people are at', but that assertion merely encourages the rejoinder '*Why* is television where the people are at?'). *Family Television* contains no attempt to work out any historical dimension to how it is that so many families have a television set. Morley gives us sociology and cultural studies without the history. And as such, it might be objected, he gives us very little at all.

By extension then, it is simply untrue to say, as Fiske does, that ethnographic studies of the audience represent something like a defeat for what he identifies as the pessimism of Frankfurt School writers like Adorno and Horkheimer. Fiske's argument is that ethnographies of watching television make it quite clear that 'The power of the people to make *their* culture out of the offerings of the culture industry' is much greater than Adorno and Horkheimer can possibly allow (Fiske 1987: 93). Fiske continues to stress his belief that, contrary to Frankfurt School conclusions, the audience is an active participant in a dialogue with the media and is therefore possessed of a 'power to reject those offerings of the culture industry which do not offer them that opportunity [that is, the opportunity to make *their* culture]' (Fiske 1987: 93).

Certainly, Fiske comes to one set of conclusions which are, in themselves, quite compatible with the evidence provided by the ethnographies of watching television. But, if it is so desired, exactly the same conclusions can be turned against themselves. They can actually be taken as decisive proof of the claim that the media have taken such a hold over the audience that the viewers really think that the decision whether to watch one television channel or another is of some importance. For Adorno and Horkheimer, of course, it is utterly irrelevant what we chose to watch or read; after all, for them, we are merely given the illusion of choice so that the grip of the culture industry can be maintained. It is perfectly possible that Morley's families represent nothing other than the extent to which the culture industry has managed to take a complete hold on all our hopes, ambitions and imaginations so that the only choice we have left – and indeed the only kind of choice we are capable of making – is whether we watch a game show on one channel or another. Fiske can use Morley to say that he is right to talk about active, resisting audiences. But it is equally possible to look at Morley's information from the perspective of Adorno and Horkheimer to validate the thesis of the passive audience of dupes. It is possible to use Morley's findings in either way without doing any kind of violence to them.

All of this is to add some detail to what I meant when I said that the ethnographic work on media audiences rather tends towards the fetishization of daily life. The ethnographic approach takes up everyday life as something complete in itself. It only asks questions about what women and men say that they do in their daily lives. But at no time is it asked why their everyday lives are like they say they are in the first place. As such, ethnographic methods cannot defamiliarize the everyday; they cannot break Martin Heidegger's hammer. Indeed, the basis of the shock of recognition which it is possible to feel when reading someone like Morley is precisely the shock of realizing that what one does oneself is done by a lot of other people as well. Morley provides comfort. He lets us believe that we might be odd but we are not *that* odd. To this extent, it might even be proposed that ethnographic findings actually assist the culture industry in its enterprise of producing a conformist and conforming audience.

The kind of research into audiences that Morley carried out is of marginal sociological significance. This is because it *explains* next to nothing. But, of course, the work of Adorno and Horkheimer can be seen as of marginal daily significance. This is because it can *describe* next to nothing.

The problem that confronts us is whether it is possible to overcome this divide; whether it is possible to combine the descriptive possibilities of ethnography with the explanatory abilities of the grand theories of Adorno and Horkheimer. It would be very nice, and for that matter very reassuring, if such a combination was indeed possible. But, unfortunately, it seems to be more sensible and appropriate to suggest that Morley on the one hand and Adorno and Horkheimer on the other are actually poles apart. It seems to be the case that it is more or less impossible, and perhaps even undesirable, to try to bring together these two very different approaches to understanding the nature of the relationship between the media and its audiences.

I believe that the work of Adorno and Horkheimer contains insights that make it possible to understand and explain the social and cultural consequences and significance of the media in new and radically disturbing ways. In other words, they do make it possible for us to carry out a sociology that manages to defamiliarize our day-to-day relationships and activities and think about them anew and for ourselves without having to accept the claims of the so-called 'experts' that they know what is truly for the best. Morley's work does none of this.

But Adorno and Horkheimer achieve all of this profound insight at the expense of talking *at* the reader rather than *to* or *with* him or her. To some extent the *Dialectic of Enlightenment* tends occasionally to be somewhat monologic. But, then again, Adorno and Horkheimer would have said that these monologic tendencies were precisely the point of the book. As Adorno and Horkheimer say in a sentence about the culture industry which is very difficult to understand at a first and even a second or a third reading (but yet again that is exactly the point they are trying to make), 'our analysis keeps to the products' inherent claim to be aesthetic images which accordingly embody truth, and demonstrates the nullity of social being in the nihilism of that claim' (Adorno and Horkheimer 1972: xvi).

It must be said in all fairness to him that Morley does not write sentences like that (although like everyone else he does have his moments of obscurity). This is the appeal of Morley's work; it is accessible. It is possible to read a book like *Family Television* and to get its point more or less immediately. Perhaps this difference between Adorno and Horkheimer and Morley is due to two factors. Firstly, perhaps it is due to attitudes towards the world. For Morley, the world is a place of popular cultural struggle and of actual or potential pleasures (not least, and most obviously, the pleasures of watching television). Meanwhile, Adorno and Horkheimer see a world of fascism and of the barbarization of humanity. Secondly, perhaps the difference is due to the fact that even though they are talking about the media, they are actually talking about rather different things. Morley is concerned to describe people's activities and practices of watching television (although, of course, what he in fact describes is what people *say* are their activities and practices). Adorno and Horkheimer are concerned to explain the grand sweep of European history. Obviously, these are two very different, and possibly even incompatible, research objects.

But, in the end, where exactly does this leave the audience? It is hard to know. Perhaps it is impossible to come up with any definite understanding of the nature of the dialogue between media texts and media audiences. Perhaps, therefore, it is impossible to reach any definite conclusion as to whether or not institutional and cultural processes mean that the dialogue is rather tending towards becoming a monologue. Perhaps it is actually impossible to say anything about the media audiences that will meet with universal acceptance and agreement precisely because the theoretical and the empirical-ethnographic approaches are so far apart if not, indeed, quite irreconcilable with each other.

For some, for those who want to know everything for sure and who want to know everything about what it is that we do, think and are, that rather vague and woolly conclusion might seem to be completely unsatisfactory. But for others, for those who carry out studies of the media and of cultural processes and trends in order to defamiliarize the familiar so that people can be shown that the world can be different than it presently is, perhaps a woolly kind of conclusion is actually a very attractive thing indeed. After all, it encourages more and more sociological work. It says that we can all do work on the media audiences without worrying about someone finding out the definite, absolute and incontrovertible truth before we do.

Chapter 4

The media and morality

Even though it is through participation in an audience that most individuals experience the media, in the final analysis it is rather hard to provide any complete appreciation of the audience. In many ways, this was the essence of the argument in the previous chapter. I was trying to make the point that if time is spent looking at how different researchers have tried to understand the audience, then it is possible to see that they tend to mean very different things when they use much the same words. On the one hand, someone like Theodor Adorno defines the audience as a passive and cretinized mass, whereas, and on the other hand, someone like David Morley sees the audience as a diverse group of active consumers. Adorno's victims are Morley's users. Both writers are talking about exactly the same people, but they come up with very different understandings of them indeed. Through the comparison of Adorno and Morley it is possible to see the very different meanings and understandings of the problem of the audience that can be developed from, respectively, a sociological and a cultural studies point of view.

Specifically, in the previous chapter I ended up reaching the conclusion that it seems to be the case that even though it is possible to have approaches which either *explain* the audience or which *describe* the audience, nevertheless it does not appear to be possible to have an approach which is capable of explaining and describing at one and the same time. The nature, constituency and activities of media audiences are, therefore, always a little enigmatic. It is possible to explain or it is possible to describe. But, by virtue of the likelihood that these two possibilities cannot usefully be brought together, there will always be something about the question of the audience that will remain unaswerable. As such, it seems to be more or less inevitable that any discussion of the audience is going to be open to doubt if not immediate rejection. But this is not a bad thing at all. It is actually a little reassuring that the media audience must always remain something of a blind-spot. Admittedly, the ambiguity of any interpretation of the audience might be unattractive to those researchers and sociologists who want to come up with the absolutely and completely true answer about everything everywhere. But, for the rest of us, perhaps it is rather helpful that it is impossible to say anything about the audience that will be able to attract and command universal consent.

On the one hand, assuming that it has been carried out in a methodologically or theoretically logical and sensible manner, it is more or less impossible for any interpretation and understanding of the audience to be proved to be definitely and conclusively wrong. So long as it is built on solid foundations, one set of conclusions about the media is essentially as valid as any other other set of conclusions. There is no necessary need to have to bow down to any of the so-called and often self-promoting experts. On the other hand, the ambiguity and incommensurability means that it actually becomes rather interesting to carry out research on media audiences. Whether it is decided to indulge in grand theory-building, or whether it is decided to conduct an ethnography of daily life and daily relationships, it is more or less inevitable that new findings will be produced. Once again, the only caveat is that the research must be carried out in a rigorous way.

A part of that rigour will involve keeping sight of the crucial point that the relationships between media texts and media audiences (whatever that relationship might be and whatever it might involve) must be understood as essentially and fundamentally *dialogical*. This is the point Voloshinov drove home. Quite simply, if it is not presumed that there is a dialogue between the media text on the one hand and the media audiences on the other, then it is difficult if not just impossible to see how the texts might be able to force some kind of answer, reply or reaction from the audience. Some of the problems which can arise if the dialogue between texts and audiences is forgotten were clearly seen in the work of Adorno and Horkheimer and Richard Hoggart. After all, they similarly argued that the media have created an audience of virtual cultural dopes who are incapable of responding to any cultural product or activity which the culture industry does not countenance and has not standardized. But they also wanted to argue that the audience is seduced by the claims of the advertisers. As I hope I showed in the previous chapter, it is more or less impossible to hold to both of these beliefs simultaneously.

But the question and the problem of audience responses to media texts is important in yet another way. It is through the media that individuals become aware of some of their moral duties towards others. Moreover, it can be argued that it is thanks to and through the media that moral concerns and moral issues are created and expressed in modern social and cultural situations. Here then, I am using the word 'moral' in a philosophical sense. With the word I am referring to the ways in which we distinguish between conduct that is right or wrong; how it is that we act and think in accordance with principles of the right and the wrong.

In this chapter I want to argue that the media are important channels through which individuals and audiences become aware of what is said to be right and wrong. I want to pursue the thought that it is through the media that individuals become aware of their obligations and duties as people who uphold the right and who condemn the wrong. This means that this chapter will be trying to open up rather new ground in the study of the social and cultural significance of the media. It also means that many of the things I say are based on arguments and speculations rather than on any body of evidence. This is because at the moment there is not really very much by way of a body of evidence or writing which could make up the material of this chapter. In other words, even if the rest of this book has not been treated as an essentially speculative piece of work, which seeks to encourage debate and thought rather than which seeks to give the right answers (whatever they might be), it is certainly the case that it is best to read this chapter as a speculation. A lot more work needs to be done on this very important question of the relationship between the media and moral values. In order to emphasize the speculative nature of much of the argument in this chapter, I will adopt a mode of address that stresses the fact that much of this represents *my* thoughts and that much of my thought is at the moment rather sketchy.

It might seem a little bit odd that I am saying that not too much research work has been carried out by sociologists or even philosophers on this thorny issue of the media and morality. After all, one of the phrases developed by sociologists which has seeped into everyday language is that of the 'moral panic'. The popularity of this phrase can be directly traced to Stanley Cohen's book, *Folk Devils and Moral Panics* which was first published in 1972. Cohen defines his terms quite nicely at the very beginning of his book. As Cohen puts the matter, 'Societies appear to be subject, every now and then, to periods of moral panic' (Cohen 1972: 9). Cohen goes on to add a little bit of flesh to this rather bare-boned statement. He writes that a moral panic can be said to have emerged when 'A condition, episode, person or group of persons emerges to become defined as a threat to societal values and interests; its nature is presented in a stylized and stereotypical fashion by the mass media' (Cohen 1972: 9). According to Cohen, these stereotypes of reporting and of the narrative construction of news stories mean that 'the moral barricades are manned by editors, bishops, politicians and other right-thinking people' (Cohen 1972: 9).

In order to provide some direction and focus for the attempts to spot a moral panic, Cohen states that 'One of the most recurrent types of moral panic in Britain . . . has been associated with the emergence of various forms of youth culture . . . whose behaviour is deviant or delinquent' (Cohen 1972: 9). He gives some examples of these forms of youth culture; Cohen talks about Teddy Boys, Hippies, Hell's Angels and, providing the raw material for his study, Mods and Rockers. Perhaps by the early 1990s, all of these stereotypes of different kinds of youth culture have led to the media image of the drug- and sex-crazed teenaged boy out on the prowl for a good time at someone else's expense.

In all of this process of the creation of moral panics, the media obviously have an absolutely central role. After all, it is through the media that a certain group or activity becomes identified as a threat to everything we are said to hold sacred. It is through the media that a moral panic is created around some activity or other. As Cohen says, the researcher 'cannot but pay particular attention to the role of the mass media in defining and shaping social problems'. After all, 'The media have long operated as agents of moral indignation in their own right . . . their reporting of certain "facts" can be sufficient to generate concern, anxiety, indignation or panic' (Cohen 1972: 16).

It should be clear that when he talks about the role of the media in moral panics, Cohen is more generally talking about how it is that some activities are labelled as deviant when others are not. What all of these concerns with deviance and images of deviance mean is that in many ways Cohen's analysis of moral panics is rather depoliticized. Cohen pays little or no attention to the possibility that moral panics might have something to do with broader social, political and economic factors than simply the nature and the meaning of deviance (broad and important though deviance is). Some of the work associated with the Birmingham Centre for Contemporary Cultural Studies tried to link up the study of moral panics with the study of political and economic issues.

The Birmingham adoption of the phrase 'moral panic' is particularly associated with the book *Policing the Crisis* (Hall *et al.* 1978). Even though the argument of *Policing the Crisis* is very complex and even though, in a typically Birmingham fashion, it shifts from empirical to theoretical claims with some rapidity, for the purposes of this discussion the main point of the book can be summarized quite easily. Stuart Hall and his colleagues were trying to explain why and how the crime of mugging was identified as a great problem in Britain during the 1970s. (Of course, the 1970s were precisely the years emphasized as a period of crisis in *The Empire Strikes Back*. To this extent, the two texts are best read as instances of the same overall project of the analysis of hegemony rather than as free-standing and wholly independent entities.) *Policing the Crisis* is particularly concerned to explore two factors: firstly, how it was that the crime of mugging was invariably identified as the special preserve and practice of black youths and, secondly, how the crisis surrounding mugging could be taken to represent a wider crisis in the legitimacy and hegemony of the British state. In the book, all of these questions and connections are explored, at least in part, through an analysis of how mugging was understood and interpreted in the media and in the law courts. The Birmingham book shows that the media reporting of mugging was very one-sided and heavily dependent upon a series of stereotypes about young urban blacks (Hall *et al.* 1978).

To a large extent then, when the Birmingham Centre for Contemporary Cultural Studies came to start talking about moral panics they simply regurgitated some of the themes of Cohen's analysis, but with the added ingredients of politics and more sophisticated theorizing.

Now, even though the work on moral panics provides a great deal of information and insight into the selection and construction of news stories by the media, it does, nevertheless, only go so far. In itself it does not tell the whole story about moral panics. This is because, despite all the other differences between them (differences which are immediately obvious if *Folk Devils and Moral Panics* is read side by side with *Policing the Crisis*), both studies only really concentrate on the production side of the media equation. They actually say very little, if not absolutely nothing, about the relationship between the media texts that create moral panics and the audiences that are, presumably, meant to be panicking. In other words, both Cohen and the Birmingham Centre are rather guilty of adopting a monologic picture of media texts and, therefore, of excluding from their work any study or comments about audiences. When they paint any picture at all of audiences, the two studies seem to assume that simply because there was a moral panic in the media there must also have been a moral panic amongst the viewers and readers.

Perhaps this is because the case studies of deviant groups or of specific forms of activity that are defined as criminal actually take a very narrow angle on what a moral panic might in fact mean. Perhaps a choice of different examples might show that if attention is taken away from crime and is instead directed towards some really big questions, then a very different picture of the relationship between the media, moral problems and morality will begin to emerge. That is exactly the point and the possibility I want to explore in this chapter. I do not want to talk about the relatively small-scale moral panics (however important and pressing they might be and become in day-to-day life and relationships). Instead, I think it might be more interesting to talk about massive issues like how it is that the media create *global* problems which evidently need some kind of moral response from us; how it is that the media operate as channels of moral value and indeed influence the very content of those values.

The obvious example of the things I am wanting to explore is the Live Aid movement of the mid-1980s. The whole basis of Live Aid was that the media, and especially the television, were able to tell stories about famine in Ethiopia which led to people in the affluent West trying to do something to alleviate the suffering in that part of Africa. To this extent then, the media were creating a moral problem of famine and forcing some kind of moral behaviour and moral reaction on the part of the audiences of those particular texts. The Live Aid movement was particularly strong in Britain and the United States. It took the form of huge rock concerts, records and fund-raising events to help alleviate the terrible famine. The movement was 'founded' by the singer Bob Geldof after he had seen television pictures of the suffering. The high point of Live Aid was a day-long rock concert which was held at Wembley Stadium in London and the John F. Kennedy Stadium in Philadelphia on 13 July 1985. The concert was broadcast throughout the world, crossing cultural and political boundaries. The concert was identified by its organizers as part of what Marshall McLuhan had called the 'global village'.

When McLuhan coined this phrase (which is explored in McLuhan and Powers 1989), he was making the point that the media have extended our ability to perceive and know different social and cultural arrangements in different places. As such, to the extent that the media have expanded what we can know, the world seems to be smaller. Thanks to and through the media we are able to live in many different worlds and cultures at the same time, without ever leaving the living room. The world has come to seem like a village. Live Aid explicitly played on this idea. The front cover to the Wembley/Philadelphia concert programme was a collage by the pop artist Peter Blake; the collage was called 'The Global Juke Box'.

It is no exaggeration to say that had it not been for the television, the whole Live Aid phenomenon would have been impossible. The power of television was absolutely central to the entire event. Indeed, the programme of the Live Aid concert was in no doubt that 'The story of the greatest rock extravaganza goes back to . . . when Bob Geldof sat at home watching a television report on the Ethiopian famine'. Here, the very ordinariness of watching television is being hinted at. The ordinariness is seen as in some way increasing the shock of what was appearing on the screen. The story continues, 'Michael Buerk and Mohamed Amin's four minute film from the feeding centres of Korem and Makele horrified Geldof' (Live Aid 1985: 12). The pictures on the screen had such an effect on Geldof that he was spurred to organize the recording of a charity record, *Do They Know It's Christmas?/Feed The World*, which sold three million copies in England alone over 1984/1985, raising £8 million for the famine relief effort. The rock concert was an attempt to capitalize on this effort.

Throughout the concert programme a great deal of emphasis is placed on the abilities and possibilities of the media. The programme also reveals a tendency to concentrate on all the technology irrespective of its uses. This might well be read as an example of another famous dictum of Marshall McLuhan: that the medium is the message. As McLuhan writes, 'In the electric age . . . our central nervous system is technologically extended to involve us in the whole of mankind and to incorporate the whole of mankind in us' (McLuhan 1964: 4). It is the technological medium of communication which changes and shapes our knowledge of the world; it is the technology which can show us certain things (such as famines) and, therefore, it is actually the medium which is of central importance. The Live Aid programme's concentration on media technology can be seen as a classic illustration of McLuhan's claim. For example, 'In Philadelphia there will be a television crew of more than 250 people, and 20 cameras. Worldwide Sports is responsible for the transmission of the two concerts around the world.' Indeed, Worldwide Sports 'Will bounce the signals off four satellites at a cost of around $200,000 – well below the normal price' (Live Aid 1985: 16). In many ways the music is much less important than the technical abilities of Worldwide Sports. Similarly, the aeroplane Concorde was also a message about the global village. Thanks to the plane, Phil Collins and a few other performers were 'able to play at Wembley, then leave for New York on Concorde at 6.30pm, arrive there at 4.30pm local time, and then get to Philadelphia at the same time they left England to play again' (Live Aid 1985: 16).

In many ways the message of the concert was not famine relief but, to paraphrase McLuhan, the media. After all, 'The two stadiums being used, Wembley and the John F. Kennedy Stadium in Philadelphia, are more than 3,000 miles apart, but are being linked by satellite in a carefully co-ordinated programme'. The broadcast 'will then go live to over 80% of the total number of television sets in existence throughout the world' (Live Aid 1985: 13).

By late 1992/early 1993 the Ethiopia region, and especially Somalia, was once again being ravaged by an awful famine. This time the situation was made considerably worse by the activities of local gangs which stole the aid that should have been getting to the starving. On 8 December 1992 troops from the United States moved into Somalia to help secure famine relief operations on behalf of the United Nations. Now what is interesting about this event is how the media took it over; indeed how the media coverage of the famine relief quickly came to be more expensive than the famine relief itself. One of the most memorable parts of the coverage of the arrival of the American troops was when the soldiers arrived on the beach near Mogadishu. The military operation had been planned to take place in the early morning so as to maximize the surprise it caused to the local gangs. However, the media were not surprised at all. They were on the beach waiting to interview the troops as they disembarked from their landing craft. According to a report by Mark Huband, the NBC network sent seventy-nine reporters and technicians to Somalia to report the troop landings. CNN had six camera crews on the beach. Huband believes that 'Media complicity in the shot-free invasion was an essential element for the mission to succeed. . . . The display of military power was the insurance against failure' (Huband 1993: 38).

Meanwhile, the ABC network rented a local villa as its headquarters and was prepared to pay so much in rent that the Save the Children Fund (one of the leading famine relief organizations) found itself unable to find offices. CBS spent $2.5 million in three weeks in Somalia (Huband 1993: 14–15). CNN spent even more money. Indeed, Mark Huband reports that 'Relief workers and CNN reporters established that the CNN coverage cost more than the entire food relief operation mounted by Care International in Baidoa, the town worst-hit by the famine where 100 people a day are dying of starvation' (Huband 1993: 38). For Mark Huband at least, the message which is communicated when we watch pictures of the starving of Baidoa is not just one of famine; it is also a message about the ability of the media to send pictures from anywhere on the globe.

Marshall McLuhan gave his own example of the effect of the media on our moral sensibilities. He argued that the social, cultural and psychological effects of television in America were demonstrated especially clearly by the funeral of John F. Kennedy. He argued that through the medium of television, the entire population of America was able to participate in the event of Kennedy's funeral. All Americans had some deep involvement in it. Thanks to the television, the funeral was invested with 'the character of corporate participation. . . . It revealed the unrivaled power of TV to achieve the involvement of the audience in a complex *process*' (McLuhan 1964: 337). McLuhan subsequently explained that 'The Kennedy funeral, in short, manifested the power of TV to involve an entire population in a ritual process. By comparison, press, movie and even radio are mere package devices for consumers' (McLuhan 1964: 337).

This is all going far beyond questions of moral panics. It is, instead, about how the media are able to influence our moral conscience. It is about how the media are able to report and create problems which are recognized as implying moral obligations on the part of the audiences. As Michael Ignatieff has said, 'Through its news broadcasts and spectaculars like "Live Aid", television has become the privileged medium through which moral relations between strangers are mediated in the modern world' (Ignatieff 1985: 57). The best possible proof that something like this actually does happen is, of course, the millions of dollars and pounds that Live Aid raised from the media audiences in such a relatively short space of time.

Michael Ignatieff is making a very important point. He is saying that most of the people in the world are strangers to one another. In other words, he is saying that we live in a world in which individuals come into contact with people who are for the most part not known in advance and who are not familiar to each other. This point is of course correct even at the most ordinary level. All that is needed to prove the point Ignatieff is making is a walk down the high street of any town or city. It is extremely likely that most of the individuals who see each other will not know or even recognize each other. To say the least, it is quite reasonable to argue that the media play an absolutely fundamental role in developing and exacerbating this sense of living in a world of strangers precisely because newspapers report stories from many different countries and television shows pictures of the people in different places. To give yet another very trite example, I know what certain places and people in Ethiopia look like even though I have never been there.

Basically, Ignatieff is trying to suggest that all of this experience of a world of strangers is of immense moral importance. Basically, newspaper reports and television pictures make us aware of people in other parts of the world. We become aware of what is happening to them. We are able to develop some kind of an awareness of what they are suffering and what they are hoping for even though the chances are that we do not personally know any single one of them. This is another dimension of the series of relationships that Marshall McLuhan was seeking to highlight with his idea of the global village.

But, even more than changing our awareness of other people in other places, Michael Ignatieff says that the media have also changed our understanding of our moral obligations towards others. That it to say, the media force us to recognize that all of the inhabitants of the global village are occupants of the same world and, therefore, tied together as if they were all neighbours (and as we all know, neighbours become good friends . . .). Ignatieff stresses the possibility that, in a case like the television coverage of the Ethiopian famine of the mid-1980s, the media can actually cut through the red tape of international politics and trade treaties and thus force people to do something in and for themselves regardless of the machinations of bureaucracies. As Ignatieff says, 'TV brought public pressure to bear upon the bureaucratic inertia, logistical stumbling blocks, and ideological excuses that had allowed a long-predicted food crisis to become a disaster' (Ignatieff 1985: 58). He continues to argue that: 'Television helped to institute a direct relation of people to people which cut through bilateral government mediations . . . it created a new kind of electronic internationalism linking the consciences of the rich and the needs of the poor' (Ignatieff 1985: 58). And so, therefore, television helped to make sure that many fewer people had to starve to death.

The great strength of Ignatieff's position is that it recognizes the important point that media texts are involved in a dialogue with media audiences. After all, when he assumes that what we watch has an impact on what we do, Ignatieff is indeed making the point that media texts inspire some kind of a response on the part of those who experience them. He might make this connection very simply, but nevertheless he does make it. In other words, Ignatieff manages to avoid falling into the trap of assuming that media texts are fundamentally monologic in their relationship with their audiences.

In these ways it is possible to make connections between the claims that are made by Michael Ignatieff and the claims of some moral philosophers. Here, I am thinking in particular of the work of Richard Rorty and his book *Contingency, Irony and Solidarity* (Rorty 1989). Admittedly, studies of the media do not talk very often about what might be called the moral dimension of media texts, and such studies talk about someone like Richard Rorty even less often. But Rorty encourages us to think about the media in very new and original ways. As such, his work manages to perform the role of helping with the defamiliarization of media texts and existing social and cultural relationships. Undoubtedly his work contains the potential to open up new directions for media research. Obviously, it is not necessary for our purposes to look at the fine detail of Rorty's argument. His book is written in a leisurely and an easy tone which rather manages to hide the immense amount of thought and reading which has gone into it. In other words, *Contingency, Irony and Solidarity* is reasonably easy to read but rather harder to understand in all its depths and complexities. For our purposes, the most important part of Rorty's argument surrounds his understanding and interpretation of what the word 'solidarity' means in moral philosophy.

When moral philosophers start talking about solidarity they are, to put the matter somewhat simply, trying to work out and explain how it is that individuals come together in unified groups and, indeed, recognize themselves as members of that group. Traditionally, moral philosophers have tried to think through this problem by emphasizing qualities like human nature or human rights, or God or nationality. The conventional response of moral philosophers is to try to explain solidarity by talking about something very large and extremely important which is held to exist beyond and often prior to our small and just a little bit trivial daily lives. In this way then, the conventional line of enquiry in moral philosophy is to try to *find* the basis of human solidarity.

For our purposes, Rorty's main claim is that it is wrong to try to *find* the basis of what it is that allegedly brings together into a unified whole all of the members of a group. He rejects the view that it is possible to go out and find the basis and meaning of solidarity. His argument is that solidarity has to be *made*. And, he says, solidarity between individuals is made when one individual is able to see other individuals as similar to themselves. In other words, solidarity is made when I am able to imagine you as similar in all important respects to me. By way of setting out his stall against what moral philosophers conventionally tend to do Rorty says that in his work, 'solidarity is not thought of as recognition of a core self, the human essence, in all human beings' (Rorty 1989: 192). This means that Rorty has to offer a different way of explaining and understanding human solidarity. He consequently says that solidarity between individuals is best thought of 'as the ability to see more and more traditional differences (of tribe, religion, race, customs, and the like) as unimportant compared with similarities with respect to pain and humiliation' (Rorty 1989: 192). What this involves is 'the ability to think of people wildly different from ourselves as included in the range of "us"' (Rorty 1989: 192). So, in these terms, there is solidarity when I argue that the differences between us of religion or of race are un-important when compared to the fact that if I can see that you suffer when you are hungry I can imagine that I would suffer too. In this way then, I am saying that even though we might appear to be very different, you and I are actually the same in all morally important respects. I stop thinking about you as 'one of them' and start thinking about you as 'one of us'.

If solidarity is something that is *made* rather than something that is *found*, then, quite simply, there have to be tools which will enable and facilitate the activities and the practices of the making. Rorty is saying that the solidarity between individuals and groups has to be made in just the same way as a house has to be made. And just as housebuilders use scaffolding, bricks and cement mixers, so those who are concerned with the problem of moral solidarity need equivalents to scaffolding and bricks. These equivalents to building equipment are to be found in places like novels, films, newspapers and television. Rorty says that it is through these different media of communication that it is possible to see that people who seem to be different to us are, in fact, actually rather similar. As such, the media are centrally understood as channels of moral discourse and, indeed, as communicators of the central moral value of solidarity. According to Rorty, the 'process of coming to see other human beings as "one of us" rather than as "them" is a matter of detailed description of what unfamiliar people are like and of re-description of what we ourselves are like' (Rorty 1989: xvi). Rorty continues to indicate who is responsible for this redescription: 'This is a task not for theory but for genres such as ethnography, the journalist's report, the comic book, the docudrama, and, especially, the novel' (Rorty 1989: xvi).

This is clearly where the media come right back into the picture and become of absolutely central concern to any study of moral value in contemporary social and cultural relationships. Perhaps Ignatieff puts the importance of the media most clearly. During his analysis of the moral implications of the media coverage of the Ethiopian famine, he comments that 'television has contributed to the breakdown of the barriers of citizenship, religion, race, and geography that once divided our moral space into those we were responsible for and those who were beyond our ken' (Ignatieff 1985: 59). For Ignatieff then, there can be little or no doubt that the medium of television has meant that all of the old barriers which kept people apart can and should now be dismantled (if they have not been dismantled already). He is saying that thanks to the television, the circle of those people for whom we feel responsible has been expanded, if only because there are very few places in the world that cannot be shown on a television screen. Consequently, it is impossible for me to say that I did not know about the Ethiopian famine, or that I did not think that anything needed to be done, because I can see how terrible the situation really is thanks to my television. Ignorance is no excuse for a lack of action. The media make sure that we are not ignorant of the suffering of other people in other parts of the world.

The kinds of claims which are made by Ignatieff and Rorty make it possible to appreciate quite how the media can take such a deep hold on so many of the things we think and so many of the things we hold to be important. But there is another side to the coin; a side which Richard Rorty for one does not seem to acknowledge. For Rorty it seems to be enough to say that the media are channels which enable us to become aware of moral problems and recognize moral responsibilities and obligations. For example, he writes in a very matter of fact way that 'the novel, the movie, and the TV program have, gradually but steadily, replaced the sermon and the treatise as the principal vehicles of moral change and progress' (Rorty 1989: xvi). This is an extremely dialogic interpretation of the significance, possibilities and impact of the media. Rorty seems to be saying that the media do not just make us aware of problems but that they also make us go into the world to try to solve the problems.

I think that what Rorty does here is fall into precisely the same kind of trap which in the end scuppered the story told by John Fiske. Fiske collapsed a statement about the possibility of oppositional readings of media texts into a statement that such readings do take place. Similarly, Rorty collapses a statement about the role of media as channels of the communication and development of moral value into a statement about the role of the media as agents of moral progress. Both Fiske and Rorty assume that because something *can* happen it therefore *does* happen. But, as I have already argued, there is absolutely no reason to argue that because something can happen it therefore does. Once again then, it is possible to perceive a blind-spot in the argument. Once again, it is possible to see an argument (or at the least a proposition) that brings together two statements which are in fact rather different. Put another way, it is most definitely the case that the media *can* play exactly the role Rorty says they can perform. They most certainly *can* be agents of moral progress and of the communication of moral value. But that should not at all directly lead to the reaching of the conclusion that the media therefore *do* perform that role. In itself, a statement about what the media can do provides no justification for a statement that the media do therefore do it.

Although I feel very moved and upset by the television pictures of naked starving and shivering children in Ethiopia, actually I do nothing – or at least very little – about it. Certainly, I do not do *enough* about it. And I am not alone in this reaction. If it was just me who was callous and heartless, if it was just me who refused to respond to the dialogic pull of the media texts, it would presumably be the case that the famine relief agencies would not have to make such desperate appeals for money. Neither would they have to make the appeals quite so frequently. So, something is going on, something is happening, which seems to imply that the possibilities which Rorty quite correctly identifies are not actually being turned into action by the media, and most definitely not by the television audiences.

In these comments, I will focus on the case of television because it is perhaps here that all of the issues and problems are thrown into the very sharpest relief. After all, it should be the case that the television has the greatest impact upon our moral sensibilities and values. But it might well be that it is actually the television that leaves the audience most cold and that results in the weakest dialogic response (notwithstanding the example of Live Aid). Thanks to the institutional nature of television, Live Aid could only be a one off. Similarly then, for the television there could only be one Kennedy funeral irrespective of the number of Kennedys who might die. These things could only happen once, because if they happen a second time they are slightly boring, and if they happen a third time, well, audience figures are likely to collapse. This paradox, which means that I am not moved to do anything, that I am not moved to respond by the pictures that upset me, has been realized and outlined by Ignatieff. In his essay on 'The Ethics of Television', Michael Ignatieff quotes with approval a suggestion by Jonathan Miller that the pictures we see on the television screen are, in themselves, incapable of *asserting* anything. In themselves, they contain no moral message except the moral message we choose to see and extract from them. This is the heart of the matter of why the upsetting pictures of the famine ultimately lead me to sit back and get fatter.

Ignatieff puts the point in a slightly jargon-riddled sentence. He says that 'The images from Ethiopia do not assert their own meaning; they can only instantiate a moral claim if those who watch understand themselves to be potentially under obligation to those they see' (Ignatieff 1985: 59). When he uses the word 'instantiate', Ignatieff is simply saying that television images can only be seen as an instance, as an example and an illustration of a moral claim if we choose to see them in that way. In themselves, the pictures and the sounds are not an illustration or an example of any single meaning (to this extent then, perhaps Ignatieff's position coincides with a Fiske-type claim that programmes only become texts with meanings when they are read by audiences).

Now, if it is accepted that media texts 'do not assert their own meaning', then it can be seen that there is nothing necessarily very strange about my personal reaction to the pictures of famines (the reaction of being very upset that people starve whilst I am eating my dinner). In particular, Ignatieff points out that the pictures and the sounds of the famine are open to two very different readings. And the moral problem is that each of the readings is as possible and as valid as the other. As Ignatieff says, 'the Ethiopian images could be interpreted in radically different ways, either as an instance of the promiscuous voyeurism a visual culture makes possible, or as a hopeful example of the internationalization of conscience' (Ignatieff 1985: 57). Obviously, quite a lot is going on in this sentence. Consequently, it will be helpful if it is unpacked a little.

What Ignatieff is claiming is that if we see pictures of the famine we can react in one of two ways. Each reaction is equally possible, and the images cannot in themselves force us to prefer one reaction as opposed to the other. That is to say, they do not instantiate their meaning. The reactions are, firstly, voyeurism and, secondly, conscience. It will be helpful to deal with each of these possible reactions in turn.

Voyeurism can be defined as an exaggerated interest in viewing certain activities or certain objects. Invariably this viewing is directed towards sexual activities and objects and it is intended to lead to sexual gratification on the part of the viewer. Now, it is possible that Ignatieff would not entirely wish to exclude a sexual dimension from his comment that there is a kind of voyeurism of the famines. But perhaps he is trying to make a much broader point about how we can seek and indeed get gratification and some pleasure from watching pictures on the television. Perhaps he is saying that we actually enjoy looking at pictures of famine precisely because they have such a mysterious appeal to us (and, therefore, it is quite likely that the appeal will be all the greater when I am sitting with a plate of food in front of me). On the bottom line it is possible to derive a kind of pleasure from the pictures because they make it possible for me to think that at least it is not me who is starving to death.

If Michael Ignatieff's suggestions are extended a little, it becomes possible to float the idea that a famine will only be considered newsworthy, and the pictures will only appear on the screen in the first place, if the famine becomes so bad that it becomes almost appealing, so bad and overwhelming that it virtually stuns any possibility of moral solidarity (Ignatieff 1985: 58). Indeed, precisely to the extent that a famine does become enormously awful, it becomes something that is understood as a tragedy made by nature rather than a tragedy made by social, economic and political relationships. It becomes something beyond our interference and intervention, just like an earthquake.

It can be speculated that this construction of awful famines as natural rather than social occurrences is symbolized in the tendency of the television pictures to show the starving naked or, at the very best, dressed in dull and tattered rags. The famine victims are presented to us as humanity reduced to the status of the 'poor bare forked animal' rather than as individuals with names, dead loved ones and crushed hopes and ambitions (to this extent there is a certain continuity with the representations of the Nazi holocaust of Jews; certainly there are many pictures of the victims of the holocaust, but the victims are invariably naked and nameless). In themselves, the pictures of the famine possibly have no social and cultural meaning; they have little or nothing by way of a value; they are just things to be looked at. This in turn raises the distinct possibility that the gaze, and therefore the moral concern, of the voyeurs who watch the television will be distracted elsewhere when there are new tragedies to watch: 'there is the suspicion that the story will drop out of the nightly bulletins when the focus upon horror shifts elsewhere in the world. The medium's gaze is brief, intense, and promiscuous' (Ignatieff 1985: 58).

The second possible reaction to the images of famine is very different to the first reaction of voyeurism. This is the reaction that Richard Rorty assumes and rather tends to place a lot of his hopes in. It is the reaction of the development of a moral conscience about the famine and a reaction of wanting to do something positive and helpful about it. This is the meaning of Ignatieff's reference to something which he calls the 'internationalization of conscience'. To quote Ignatieff yet again, 'Millions of households look out through the screen in search of their collective identity as a national society and as citizens of one world' (Ignatieff 1985: 71). He continues in a way that can be read as a direct anticipation of what Rorty has to say: 'The media now play the decisive role in constituting the "imagined community" of nation and globe, the myth that millions of separate "I's" find common identity in a "we"' (Ignatieff 1985: 71).

But there is something by way of a sting in the tail of Ignatieff's ruminations on the implications for morality and moral concern of the medium of television. The sting becomes apparent when Ignatieff begins to think about the institutional context of the pictures of famines in Ethiopia. He stresses the nature and the requirements of the news programmes which are the primary source of the images of the famines. Ignatieff argues that television news operates in terms of the convention that something can only be called news if there are pictures of it and if it can be contained within very small time slots (ranging from a few seconds to an hour at the very most). This means that any given news programme will contain a whole mixture of pictures and stories, each of which jostles with the others to become memorable, each of which is turned into something which is only *relatively* important (so that, for example, the famine in Ethiopia is more important than the collapse of a bridge in Turkey because the famine is the headline; but tomorrow the famine might well be less important than the latest stage of debates on economic policy in Europe).

For Ignatieff, all of this means that news is not just 'promiscuous' but that it is also incoherent. This tendency towards the incoherence of television news programmes is exacerbated by the tendency of many of the news programmes to contain lengthy but more or less trivial human interest items. Ignatieff writes of news programmes that 'this jumble of events is presented to the viewer as if it were a representation of the promiscuity of the external world' (Ignatieff 1985: 71). He goes on to comment that the 'redefinition of news value to include the curious, bizarre, and the entertaining has destroyed the coherence of the genre itself' and so audiences are forced to 'ask themselves at least once a night, "Why am I being shown this? Why is this news?"' (Ignatieff 1985: 71).

The nub of the paradox which Michael Ignatieff identifies is this. On the one hand, television has the potential to act as a channel for the communication of moral value which can therefore and thereby force a possibly practical recognition of moral responsibilities towards people about whom barely a thought was previously given. In other words, thanks to the abilities of television it becomes potentially possible for the groups and the constituencies of the 'us' to see 'them' as actually like 'us' in all significant respects. So far so good; so far so much like Richard Rorty. But, on the other hand, Ignatieff stresses the institutional context of the pictures of famine and suffering. He stresses the importance of the point that the pictures are usually shown as news items in news bulletins. As such, they are compressed in time and they are reduced to the level of being just one instance of suffering in a whole gallery of horrors or weird and wonderful incidents. Put another way, if we do not like one particular story we need not pay too much attention to it because we know that it will go away in a few minutes. Consequently, the moral impact of the television images is minimized if not trivialized by the institutional context in which the images are broadcast.

In many ways, these problems which Ignatieff outlines can be backed up by ethnographic studies of what people say it means to watch television news. Now, I am not using ethnographic material to try to validate Ignatieff's more abstract reflections on the relationship between the media and morality. Neither am I using ethnographic material when it supports the case I want to make even though I reject it when it does not fit my story quite so neatly. I maintain that ethnographic research can only lead to *descriptions* of how the media are used and that, in itself, ethnography explains very little if not absolutely nothing. All I am wanting to do here is provide another way of looking at the relationship between the media, moral problems and the communication and making of moral values.

Here then, I want to discuss some ethnographic research which Klaus Bruhn Jensen has carried out on how media audiences say that they make sense of television news broadcasts. In his own terms at least, Jensen can help to describe what it actually means to watch the news (Jensen 1992). As with David Morley's work, it is possible to have very major doubts about the usefulness of Jensen's research sample. Indeed, Jensen's sample is even narrower than Morley's: 'the sample, drawn from a local university directory, represented two groups of twelve male full-time teaching and research staff and twelve males in various service or administrative positions' (Jensen 1992: 220). Jensen's ethnography revolves around twenty-four interviews about twelve news broadcasts. The 'interviews were recorded in a metropolitan area of the northeastern United States during three randomly selected weeks in the autumn of 1983' (Jensen 1992: 220).

What Jensen found was that the people he interviewed watched the news in very different ways and for very different reasons. It is the set of reasons which concern us. Certainly, these findings seem to suggest that from an ethnographic point of view it is not terribly legitimate to say that news broadcasts mean any single thing to all the viewers. Once again, then, we are left talking about audiences in the plural as opposed to an audience in the singular. Jensen argues that the different respondents constituted different audiences which used news broadcasts in a variety of different ways: 'The term "uses" is employed to refer to that broad range of social, familial and individual relevances which viewers

ascribe to news and other media genres' (Jensen 1992: 224). He identified four main uses: contextual, informational, legitimating and diversional uses. It will be helpful to explain each of these categories in turn.

When he talks about *contextual uses*, Jensen is referring to the social
and cultural environments in which the news is watched. He is trying to
describe how watching the news puts down time-markers in the daily
routines of family and domestic life. Jensen discovered that 'News-
viewing may . . . be seen as overdetermined by the roles and routines of
family life; it is an integrated element of the evening context in the
home' (Jensen 1992: 225). In other words, the way we watch the news
will be influenced in a very fundamental way by our roles and position
in the family. This is a point that Dorothy Hobson, Tania Modleski and
David Morley have all made as well. Jensen notes that news viewing
was often associated by his respondents with cooking or eating food.
The point is of course that the person who eats the food is more able to
concentrate on the news broadcast than the person who is cooking the
food. Moreover, watching the news is identified as the beginning of the
evening leisure time of the (invariably male) 'breadwinner', whereas for
the (invariably female) worker in the home it is just one more moment
in the daily routine of domestic labour. Consequently, 'it comes out that
family members do not have equal opportunity to watch the news,
because the gendered roles and relations of power in the family also
apply to media uses' (Jensen 1992: 225).

Secondly, Jensen talks about the *informational uses* of news broadcasts. He says that, 'We may define the informational dimension of
news . . . as factual knowledge of political issues and events which is
relevant to viewers in a context of social action' (Jensen 1992: 226). In
other words, we watch the news to find out what is happening in the
world around us; what ministers are doing now to make our lives just
that little bit more miserable.

Thirdly, there are the *legitimating uses* of news viewing. Here,
Jensen is trying to describe how we watch the news in order to place
ourselves in the wider world. Jensen is saying that we use the television
news to understand ourselves and our place in the scheme of things. This
is achieved by using the media to locate us in terms of political issues.
As Jensen expresses this aspect of the use of television news broadcasts:
'the media address recipients' *social* identity and, further, that social
identity is specifically associated with issues of political life'. Jensen
continues: 'News-viewing, then, is less a matter of exploring one's
personal identity in the abstract than of situating oneself in relation to a
range of concrete political concerns' (Jensen 1992: 229).

Finally, Jensen identifies the *diversional uses* of the news. Here, he is making the point that even though his respondents identified television news as about politics, they also saw it as something that could offer diversions from the problems and boredom of everyday life. The respondents identified the diversionary capacities of the news with two main qualities. Firstly, the news could offer a diversion if the newsreader (that is, the 'anchor') combined professional competence with personal appeal. Inevitably, this has definite gender overtones: 'Recasting the anchors as glamorous objects, rather than subjects of a discourse on politics, the male respondents evidently derive a variety of visual pleasures from watching TV news' (Jensen 1992: 233). But news could be diverting in a second way. The news could be diverting if the pictures it showed and the graphics it used were interesting and exciting. Here, it would seem that Jensen's respondents might well be talking about much the same things as Michael Ignatieff when he commented on the voyeuristic dimensions of watching pictures of the Ethiopian famine. Jensen says that 'the respondents refer to the visuals of news events as an attraction in their own right. The images offer great variety, and may be used as an occasional diversion from house chores and other work' (Jensen 1992: 233).

Now, if it is indeed argued that there is some relationship between the media (and especially television news broadcasts) and the identification of and response to, moral problems, then two assumptions need to be made. The argument that there is a connection between the media and morality can only really work if it is assumed that two processes exist and are in operation. Firstly, it has to be assumed that media texts and media audiences participate in dialogic relationships. Arguably, this assumption is well founded and perfectly justifiable in terms of both the desire to explain through theory and describe through ethnography the social and cultural significance of the media. There seems to be no very great problem in accepting this assumption (even though the nature of that dialogue, and the negotiations and relationships of power within it, might well be open to considerable doubt and investigation. After all, Adorno and Horkheimer could be seen to be occupying the rather paradoxical space of contending that the dialogue carried out between the culture industry and the audience actually tends towards a monologue).

However, the second assumption is somewhat more difficult to accept. Basically, if it is argued that television news is indeed a channel of moral concerns and actions and of the communication of moral value, then it must also be assumed that the television news is taken *seriously* by the audiences. It must be assumed that everyone watches the news to get direct and what is assumed to be objectively true information about the world beyond the front door. It must also be assumed that the audiences all watch the news attentively so that they are in a position to understand and respond properly to the great moral issues of the day. It is this second series of assumptions which is more than a little bit doubtful. On the one hand, Ignatieff points out that there is a fundamental ambivalence about what television news images might mean. Furthermore, and on the other hand, the ethnographic research of Jensen indicates that the news is just as likely to be watched for a bit of fun as it is to be watched for information about what is happening in the world.

In other words, there is no basis upon which it can be taken for granted that the audiences watch the news with the kind of moral seriousness and commitment that a moral philosopher like Richard Rorty presupposes.

But perhaps there is even more to this problem than work such as that carried out by Ignatieff and Jensen can allow. Perhaps it is the case that as we become more and more familiar with the pictures of incidents and processes which possibly should inspire a moral response on our part, our ability to respond to them in any positive way actually lessens and lessens. What I am trying to say is that it is possible to speculate that as we become ever more aware of famines in various parts of the world, as we turn on the television and are forced to confront once again the horror of starvation, we actually become desensitized to the enormity of it all. Perhaps the very success of the media in being able to tell us so much about the world actually diminishes our ability to act in the world. Not only do pictures of famines become a little bit tedious – what is another starving child when you have seen pictures of one already this week? – but also pictures of famines become just another part of the fabric of the world – what would we have to moan about if there was not a famine in Ethiopia or Somalia or Mozambique or wherever? What exactly would Europe be about if it was not able to prevaricate over a response to mass rape in Bosnia? Consequently, perhaps the media are incapable of having the moral impact Rorty assumes they have because the audiences become *anaesthetized* to media images.

I want to argue that when it comes to an analysis of the identification of moral problems and the communication of moral values, the media and especially television news can usefully be understood as operating as a kind of anaesthetic. In particular, the only real conclusion that can be drawn from Ignatieff and from the ethnography of Jensen is that the format of the television news induces in the audiences a loss of the possibility of the sense of shared pain and suffering, a loss of the sense of empathy, which is possibly communicated by the news pictures. In other words, it seems to be the case that the dominant and most obvious media format of the identification of moral problems (that is, news broadcasts) actually manages to destroy the chance that anything can be done about those problems. This anaesthetic effect has three parts.

Firstly, it is due to the fact that the audiences build up a tolerance towards pictures of famine and suffering. Pictures have to become ever more shocking to have any impact on us, but if the pictures are too shocking it is likely that we will go and make a cup of tea instead of having to endure them.

This possibility leads to the second aspect of the anaesthetic effect. Quite simply, it is possible that there will be so much suffering on the screen that the audiences will find themselves to be incapable of doing anything at all about it. It is possible that a news broadcast could be so horrible that instead of suggesting some kind of dialogic response it might, rather, become something more by way of a monologue of the woes of the world. The news might make us morally exhausted and weary as opposed to morally excited and active. Quite a good sense of this possibility of moral exhaustion is contained in the autobiography of the largely forgotten mid-twentieth-century writer Stefan Zweig. Zweig's life in many ways represents the career of twentieth-century Europe: he was born into a highly cultured Jewish family in Vienna, became an author of novels, stories and libretti for operas but was forced into exile when the Nazis moved into Vienna in the 1930s. He subsequently left Europe and committed suicide with his wife in Brazil in November 1942. Zweig saw himself as someone who was trapped by the movements of his day and his sense of the trap was exacerbated by the media. At the beginning of his autobiography, Stefan Zweig reflects on how he became aware of the horrors of his time. As Zweig says, 'When bombs laid waste the houses of Shanghai, we knew of it in our rooms in Europe before the wounded were carried out of their homes' (Zweig 1943: 8). He continues: 'What occurred thousands of miles over the sea leaped bodily before our eyes in pictures. There was no protection, no security against being constantly made aware of things and being drawn into them' (Zweig 1943: 8). Thanks to the media, this is an almost complete exhaustion because it is an almost complete imprisonment within horror.

Thirdly, the anaesthetic effect is due to the nature of news programmes; the most disturbing items are framed by what are possibly the most trivial items. As such, the enormity of the horrors in a famine zone are likely to be diminished if not utterly forgotten about as soon as the news item changes.

In all of these ways, then, it is perhaps necessary to be very cautious about Richard Rorty's claim that television, and the media more broadly, are now amongst the most important channels through which we learn about moral problems and think through the question of human solidarity. At an extremely grand and possibly rather abstract level, Rorty's position is undoubtedly correct and stimulating. But at the mundane level of what it actually means to watch television, and at the level of what a television picture actually means in itself, the situation is in no way as clear cut and definite as Rorty might want to have us believe. It is not necessarily the case that the pictures on our television screens and the stories in our books are capable of adding anything at all to the course of moral progress.

Yet there is even more to the matter than this. So far, I have only raised questions about how audiences respond to what they see or read. The major difficulty here is that it is almost certainly the case that many issues which are, or which could be, of moral concern never come before our eyes and ears because, for one reason or another, they are not considered to be news. It might even be said that there is a profound moral problem which revolves around the fact that the institutional operation of the media might mean that some issues will never be recognized as moral problems. To put all of this by way of a question: is something a problem if it is not reported in the news? Does Ethiopia cease to be a problem when it falls out of the headlines because the situation in Sarajevo is identified as more serious and more pressing (and because the pictures from Sarajevo are much more exciting)?

This is all to raise questions about the social and cultural relationships of power that create moral problems. But, as political and social theorists have known for some time now, it is possible that power consists in not just having your own way, but also in making sure that certain issues never become identified as problems that need to be dealt with. With this point I am alluding to the work which Peter Bachrach and Morton S. Baratz carried out on decision-making procedures in political institutions. Obviously, in view of their concerns it is rather difficult, if not utterly misplaced, to want to apply Bachrach and Baratz directly to any study of the media. But it seems to me that they can help with the development of an understanding and an interpretation of why and how it is that some issues are never identified as moral problems by and in the media.

In their book *Power and Poverty* (Bachrach and Baratz 1970), Bachrach and Baratz explain that it is possible for institutions to operate in such a way that decisions never have to be made on certain issues. They call this *non-decision making* and explain that a non-decision is 'a means by which demands for change in the existing allocation of benefits and privileges in the community can be suffocated before they are even voiced' (Bachrach and Baratz 1979: 44). They are saying that within institutions there are likely to be relationships of power which mean that some problems never reach a stage where a decision will have to be made about them. Similarly, it is possible to speculate that media institutions might well operate in such a way so that certain issues never come before the audiences and are, therefore, never capable of becoming moral problems. If any work is carried out on the relationship between the media and moral problems, it is vitally important that it pays a great deal of attention to the kinds of issues raised by Bachrach and Baratz. Rorty's concerns, and for that matter even the arguments of Ignatieff and Jensen, can take absolutely no account of the possibility that there might well be a question to be asked about how it can be that some things are never identified or recognized as moral problems requiring some kind of moral response. All they can talk about are the implications and the significance of what audiences see, hear or read. More or less by definition they cannot talk about the significance of what is *not* put before the audiences (nor can they even explain in any great detail how the standards of significance are devised in the first place within media institutions). But Bachrach and Baratz do have something very important to say about this issue; something which can be used to raise research questions and guide research inquiries.

As such, if any research is going to be carried out around this very tricky but immensely important issue of the relationship between the media and morality, then attention will also have to be paid to considerably broader social and cultural relationships. It will have to look beyond the media in isolation. Any research along these lines will have to be built on the claim that the media actually cannot be seen in isolation, actually cannot be removed from a broader social and cultural context. That is to say, any analysis of the media and morality will not just focus on the dialogue between texts and audiences (as Ignatieff and Jensen rather tend to suggest), it will also concentrate on the complex relationships between the media and questions and attributions of *value*. In that way, it might well become possible to develop an understanding of two areas of social and cultural life. Firstly, it might be possible to understand exactly what it is that the media have done to moral values. It might become possible to explain precisely how it is that in the situation where technology promises the making of the greatest possible solidarity between humans, all that actually results is a kind of moral boredom and dullness. Secondly, it might be possible to understand how and why it is that media audiences are in the last instance so unconcerned about the goodness or badness of what they see, do and like.

Chapter 5

The silence

In the previous chapter I posed and explored the problem that even though the media, and especially television, could reasonably be assumed to be some of the major and most influential channels for the making of moral solidarity between ourselves and others, the very forms of the organization and the reception of the media meant that their content could never, in fact, have that profoundly moral effect. Indeed, it seems to be the case that the more that terrible events are shown on the screen, or the more that terrible events are reported in the press, then the less of an impact they are able to have upon us. The terribleness becomes banal. Consequently, it was hinted that it is quite likely that the media do not serve so as to sensitize us to moral problems. Quite the contrary; the media rather tend to have an *anaesthetic effect.*

The previous chapter led to and can sustain only one conclusion: despite the common-sense validity of Richard Rorty's faith in the possibility that the media can operate as channels of the communication of moral values (and by extension as channels for the making of moral solidarity), an analysis of the media rather throws that validity into doubt. Quite simply, there does not seem to be any completely persuasive reason to believe that solidarity can be made in the ways that Richard Rorty proposes. Instead of promoting the development and the enhancement of the possibility of solidarity between 'us' and 'them', the media drastically and possibly even irrevocably prejudice it. The case can be put much more strongly yet. It is perhaps not unreasonable to suggest that the media mean the destruction of the moral values of solidarity.

Indeed, on the strength of the discussion around themes raised by Rorty, the only justifiable conclusion that can be reached would seem to be one which is in many ways heavily reminiscent of the lessons Theodor Adorno tried to teach. It does not seem to be entirely impossible that Adorno's essentially cultural critique of the media can be expanded into a moral critique also. The media do not raise their audiences to new levels of humanity, solidarity and cultural sophistication. The media make us lazy cowards who are incapable of willing, or for that matter incapable even of feeling any need to imagine, any kind of enlightenment. Once again, then, the argument returns to a version of the dialectic of enlightenment and, rather more specifically, to a consideration of the fate of Kant's call for humanity to use its own understanding of the order of things and thus freely make the world a 'better place' (Kant 1970). (In Rorty's terms, the world can be made a better place to the extent that it is possible imaginatively to recognize ever more similarities or identities between 'us' and 'them'. Progress consists in that ever-increasing recognition. Clearly, this version of the word 'progress' has no teleological connotations. Rorty's use of 'progress' does not imply some process that aims towards arrival at some definite goal which can be known in advance.)

Rorty's belief that the media can be channels for the making of moral solidarity is, to some extent, predicated precisely on a kind of Kantian notion that it is possible for us independently to think for ourselves and thereafter act in terms of those understandings. Kant wanted all of this coming together of ideas and practices to happen so that humanity could be freed from the intellectual shackles of superstition and knowledges imposed as if from outside. Rorty wants it to happen so that ever-more universal meanings of humanity might be made, constructed and practised in everyday relationships. (Despite this identification of similarities which connect Kant and Rorty, it should nevertheless be stressed that Rorty is highly critical of the foundations of Kant's moral philosophy, and especially the Kantian foundation of the assumption of a universal humanity which is simply waiting to be found. For the distance between Kant and Rorty see especially Rorty's comments at the end of *Contingency, Irony and Solidarity* (Rorty 1989). But this ontological disagreement does not invalidate the identification of some possible narrative similarities between their work.)

Rorty assumes that the media can enable us imaginatively to construct bonds of moral solidarity. He assumes that the media can be channels through which bonds can be freely and wilfully made independently of what we are otherwise told or inclined to believe (this is one of the points Michael Ignatieff was also trying to make when he stressed the way in which the television pictures of the famine in Ethiopia were able to cut through the restrictions imposed by bureaucratic rationalities). In this way it can be proposed that Rorty basically presupposes an ability on the part of the media to operate as the means of a moral enlightenment. He assumes a deeply dialogical relationship between media texts and media audiences. The preceding chapter tried to show that Rorty's faith might not be entirely well founded. It could more probably be the case that the media actually prevent and hinder the making of solidarity. That which should *enable* the making of solidarity in fact more likely manages to *prevent* it.

Of course, it could be objected that the discussion of these issues was so speculative as to be almost facile. In this chapter I want to try to overcome that objection by, in the first instance, offering what might be treated as a case study of what realistically can only be seen as the far from desirable relationship between the media and moral value. I propose that the difficulties with Rorty's faith in the media go rather beyond the issues of audience reception and moral anaesthesia (vitally important though those questions are). I propose that the media's ability to reproduce images more or less without end means that the possibility that media images might operate as channels of moral solidarity is rendered increasingly improbable. The increasing *quantity* of the media's technologically reproduced images of others goes hand in hand with the decreasing moral *quality* of those very images.

I suggest that this paradox is expressed most clearly in Andy Warhol's paintings of Jackie Kennedy and especially in the *Jackie* of 1964 (which is housed in the Museum of Modern Art, Frankfurt-am-Main. The painting is reproduced in Shanes 1991: 101). The *Jackie* I want to discuss is made up of thirty-five individual canvasses each of which is a silkscreen reproduction in black and grey (or perhaps, rather, in shades of grey) of a photograph of Jackie Kennedy. The original press photograph that Andy Warhol used for this particular image of Jackie was taken on board the presidential plane on the evening after John F. Kennedy had been assassinated in Dallas. In the photograph, Jackie Kennedy's face is shown side on; her expression seems to be one of a complete emptiness (in so far as any definite and single meaning at all can be read into the expression). The painting is one of a series of representations of Jackie Kennedy which Warhol made over the period 1964–6.

Indeed, with this shift from a concentration on the operation and the images of the media which Rorty inspires, to a more explicit concern to investigate the qualities and resonance of a specific work of art, it is also possible to bring together the threads of the argument developed in this book and show how it is quite possible (or at least not entirely impossible) that the fates of cultural and moral values are not divisible but, instead, are rather more likely to be similar and to go hand in hand. One of the great insights of Richard Rorty's work is that he can make it possible for analysis to overcome the common argument that art and morality occupy different and even quite incommensurable spheres of social and cultural activity. Rorty shows that art and morality might have, or might be made to have, a great deal in common. Thanks to Rorty it is not unreasonable to contend that representations (be they on the television screen, in newspapers or in art galleries), can be vitally important media for the making of moral solidarity between 'us' and 'them'.

A reading inspired by Richard Rorty would suggest that Andy Warhol's representation of Jackie Kennedy is, or at the least most certainly could be, of the utmost significance for the making of moral solidarity. According to this kind of approach, it should be possible for the spectator to look at the painting and then use it as a resource in order to make some statement about the invalidity of previously accepted divisions between 'us' and 'them'. The painting would thus be a tool for a making of solidarity. That solidarity would presumably be about empathy with the grief of the survivor when a loved one is killed, or about empathy with the young widow whose life has been destroyed by a sniper's bullet. Presumably, in a Rorty-type reading, the spectator would be expected to realize and possibly even know beforehand that Jackie is not just a figure in a painting, in a photograph or on the television screen but that she is a feeling individual of great historical and symbolic importance. According to this approach, then, the spectator will be able to use the picture as a way of understanding that Jackie is 'one of us' who hurts when someone close dies.

In the terms implied by a Rorty-type reading, it could also be speculated that the enormity of the suffering of Jackie is itself represented in Warhol's painting by the fact that the grieving face (which Warhol turns from an individual item into a symbolic form; from the grieving face to the face of grief) appears not once but thirty-five times. Once is not enough to convey the full meaning of the emotion implied by the picture. Indeed, the very repetition of the image of Jackie could be interpreted as a magnification of the grief caused by the assassination of the President and an attempt to come to terms with its quality through quantity. The point is that even though each of the thirty-five pictures looks the same at first glance, Warhol's use of the silkscreen technique means that each image is actually slightly different from any other; thicknesses of paint vary, different blotches appear in different places as the silkscreen clogs with paint. It is possible to argue that these slight differences within repetition tend to make *Jackie* far more moving than it might have been if the photograph had been reproduced just once.

Perhaps this effect of Warhol's repetition of images can be likened to the effect of hearing repetition in music. John Cage has discussed a performance of a piece of music by Erik Satie. The performance consisted of the same piece of music being played over and over again for eighteen hours. Cage says that 'if you hear something said ten times, why should you hear it anymore? But the funny thing was it was never the same twice' (quoted in Stein 1982: 191). Cage continues to say that the effect of hearing the same piece of music being played for eighteen hours was eventually very moving and profound: 'I was surprised that something was put into motion that changed me. I wasn't the same after that performance as I was before. The world seemed to have changed' (quoted in Stein 1982: 191–2). Certainly, John Cage for one was happy to suggest that the impact of the music of Satie bears direct comparison with the impact of the art of Andy Warhol. According to Cage, just like Satie, 'Andy has fought by repetition to show us that there is no repetition really, that everything we look at is worthy of our attention. That's been the major direction for the twentieth century, it seems to me' (quoted in Stein 1982: 192).

A Rorty-type reading would seize upon John Cage's understanding of the effect of Warhol's use of repetition. After all, Cage is saying, or at the very least he is heavily implying, that media-generated images can, in effect, be the basis of a new consciousness of the world and of one's self in the world. This is precisely the kind of transformation (a transformation that occurs originally in the realm of ideas but then moves out into the world of material practices) that Rorty would want to emphasize as a possibility if not indeed an absolute necessity in the making of moral solidarity.

But perhaps *Jackie* is not as straightforward as that. Perhaps it illustrates nothing other than the amorality of technological reproductions and, by extension, the impossibility of the media being or becoming anything as important or insistent as channels of moral discourse. John Coplans has hinted at this kind of possibility. Coplans points to the moral ambivalences of the use of photographs in Warhol's art. He says that 'Photographs of faces are supposed to be revealing of more than the physical structure of the face. However they rarely reveal inner truths about the person concerned' (Coplans n.d: 52). (The moral importance of the face of the other is stressed to greatest effect by Emmanuel Levinas and Susan Sontag: see Levinas 1988; Sontag 1991.) But Coplans quickly pulls himself back from the uncertainties of the ambivalence of the photograph; he refuses to follow his line of inquiry to its logical conclusion. Instead, he uses the ambivalence contained in Andy

Warhol's use of photographs for his own purposes. From it, he, perhaps desperately and certainly rather curiously, extracts a definite meaning: 'That is why the *Jackie* paintings are so powerful (and touch us so deeply). Mrs Kennedy may have been photographed during a terrible experience or ritual, but in the Warhol paintings she looks normal even in anguish' (Coplans n.d: 52).

But since the images of Jackie are themselves vacant and incapable of instantiating anything definite and single in and for themselves, something which Coplans acknowledges when he says that she looks 'normal', it is more valid to propose that, instead of moving the spectator, *Jackie* rather more has the impact of leaving the spectator quite cold and unmoved. The image is fundamentally amoral because it possesses little or nothing by way of the authority or integrity of authenticity which could sustain a making of moral solidarity in terms of it. Warhol's painting is itself a reproduction of a representation of a reproduction of a representation (after all, Warhol does not reproduce the original photograph of *Jackie*; what he reproduces is the newspaper photograph of Jackie). Consequently, Warhol's picture possesses nothing by way of an Adornoesque aura which might lend it some force of compulsion. As Richard Morphet has usefully written: 'Their images already drained of freshness by publicity or ubiquity . . . people and objects appear in Warhol's work at two removes' (Morphet 1971: 13). Furthermore, 'Rather than directly confronting person or object in his painting process by striving to capture their likeness, Warhol is loosely transposing pre-existing marks from one state into another' (Morphet 1971: 13–14). In these terms, Warhol provides a representation of a world of the technological (media) reproduction of images and art. He offers none of the critique of the present or search for the ineffable – he offers none of the space for interpretation and different meanings – which a tool of the making of moral sensibility would require. Warhol confirms the status of 'them' as 'them'. A painting like *Jackie* does not at all help to pull the subject Jackie into the community of the 'one of us'.

Jackie can be seen as an expression of the fate of the possibility of the making of moral solidarity when images of others are gained solely or invariably through the media. The media have caused the emergence of a moral and cultural world where images are technologically reproduced to such an extent that their original conditions of existence and authority are quite destroyed or are at best made of little more than anecdotal interest. That is why, contrary to John Coplans, *Jackie* actually is not a moving representation of grief. In itself the picture says and means nothing. It has no moral depth. There are at least three ways in which

Jackie is an amoral picture. Firstly, it actually *reduces* the enormity and the suffering of grief. Secondly, the painting is *passive* and therefore a representation of a *natural* occurrence about which it is possible to do absolutely nothing, rather than *active* and therefore a representation of a *social and cultural occurrence* of pressing moral significance. Thirdly, and as an extension of the second aspect, *Jackie* is an icon since it isolates the image of *Jackie* from any context; Warhol's painting has no historical situation. Each of these aspects needs to be discussed in turn and in some detail.

At a first glance, it would seem to be the case that Andy Warhol's repetition of the photograph of Jackie should serve to magnify and deepen the grief of both Jackie and the spectator alike. To this extent, it could be suggested that Warhol's repetition of one single photograph is an attempt to create an image that is big enough and powerful enough to represent such a deep and great personal emotional trauma as the murder of a loved one and such a profound national trauma as the murder of a young president. But the formal qualities of the picture mean that such a magnification is impossible. The reproduction diminishes rather than increases the moral and the emotional quality of the representation. Warhol's picture is extremely rythmical; the alternation of the pale grey of Jackie's face with the darker grey (going on black) of her hair means that the painting looks like a series of diagonal stripes going from the top left of the canvas to the bottom right corner. The eye of the spectator is drawn *across* the painting instead of *into* it. The painting encourages a kind of visual strolling and at best loitering instead of any kind of standing still and contemplating. The painting inspires a detached move-ment as opposed to an involved staying still. And if the making of moral solidarity requires anything it requires a sense of involvement on the part of the audience. Without a sense of involvement the representations would not matter. They would not be able to force any kind of disruption of the pre-existing and possibly even accepted-since-time-immemorial divisions of 'us' and 'them'.

Furthermore, each of the thirty-five faces of Jackie loses any indivi-duality it might have possessed (despite the differences within repeti-tion). Instead, each face takes a place in the panoply of faces and becomes little more than a grey smudge. The very repetition of the faces means that the individual face (the *individual* face which according to Levinas makes moral demands in and of its own and has a compelling authority in itself), is in fact, effaced in the gaze of the spectator. The structure of Warhol's painting means that the spectator actually does not concentrate upon it and cannot therefore use it for any sustained contemplative purpose (such as the making of moral solidarity). The spectator is overwhelmed by the number of Jackies to such an extent that concentration on any single Jackie is made more or less impossible. Jackie ceases to be an individual person with feelings; the face of Jackie loses its moral authority, authenticity, integrity and aura. Instead, *Jackie* becomes a genre of blank and empty suffering. As if in a vicious circle from which there is no escape, Warhol creates a *Jackie* who suffers; and suffering thereby becomes the meaning of *Jackie*. There is nothing more which can be said because the picture creates no space from which the saying might be possible.

Secondly, Warhol's painting is amoral because it pictures an event without history. By reproducing publicly available media images of Jackie Kennedy, Warhol's painting actually takes Jackie out of the social, cultural and moral worlds. Jackie is turned into a passive object (turned into something resembling a natural fact) rather than an active subject. As Richard Morphet has noted, 'Most of Warhol's people and objects either simply exist, enigmatically . . . or even, more characteristically, *have things done to them*' (Morphet 1971: 18). (Note how Morphet finds it perfectly acceptable to talk about Warhol's objects and people in exactly the same sentence.) Jackie is dehumanized; *Jackie* is a testament and an expression of that dehumanization. She is an object of suffering and an object which suffers. In no way does Warhol's painting offer a commentary on *why* Jackie has the expression she has and neither, for that matter, does the painting offer any sort of commentary on why this picture of this woman is at all important. The painting indicates no event of which it can therefore be the record. It is, instead, simply a registration of an appearance that lacks any kind of authority or right to speak in and for itself. Once again, *Jackie* actually says and means nothing. The painting merely records without comment, much like the camera that took the original photograph which was reproduced in the newspaper only to be reproduced in turn by Warhol.

This is all very significant. Cultural and moral events are indeed things which are constructed and understood as *happening*. They are interpreted in terms of chains of cause and effect, and are invariably explained through the use of a narrative which obeys the structural requirement of having a beginning, middle and an end. Cultural and moral life is generally apprehended as a story (or at least as something about which stories can be written. Sociology represents one kind of story telling; a story telling which tries desperately to forget its status as a story and which instead masquerades as something which is called 'objective scientific truth'). In his own way, Richard Rorty is concerned to tell and inspire new stories about how it is that individuals come to recognize their solidarity with others. But with its simple registration of passivity, *Jackie* is pushed outside of any narratives. *Jackie* is a painting which has no tale to tell; it just *is*. To this extent, *Jackie* is something which confronts cultural and moral life as if from the outside. It is isolated and sufficient unto itself. It is without a history and therefore without any compelling social and cultural meaning.

It is but a short step from this point to the third aspect of the amorality of *Jackie*. To the extent that the painting takes the image outside of social, cultural and moral narratives, and to the extent that it has no necessary emotional content (that is, to the extent that it means nothing), *Jackie* is an icon. The painting is complete in itself and leaves no space for interpretation or for the attribution of meanings. Indeed, the qualities of the painting serve to undermine and disqualify it as a channel of the making of moral solidarity virtually even before any making might have been embarked upon. Just as *Jackie* says nothing because Jackie says nothing, so absolutely nothing is left to be said. The image is complete in itself and broaches no argument. It exists; that is all.

As Andy Warhol's *Jackie* shows and illustrates so well, the ability of the media (in the first instance) to reproduce images rather flies in the face of the moral authority of those very images. Certainly, the media mean that images can be freed from the time and place of their original and authentic existence so that they can become full parts of everyday relationships, but, in the process, the images cease to have any meaning and integrity of their own. They definitely cease to be able to sustain anything as ambitious and important as a making of moral solidarity. In becoming freed from what Walter Benjamin would have seen as the obsolescence and the rituals of the galleries, images also become freed from meaning and importance. It could even be said that the more images are used (and Walter Benjamin was of course quite right – the use can indeed be political; following Bennett and Hall it can even be said that images can become props in the construction of new consti-tuencies of 'the people' and in new formations of popular culture), the more they become morally useless. Perhaps Adorno was right after all to bewail the impact of the culture industry.

Once again, the anaesthetic effect emerges. The meaning, importance and value of any single image becomes drastically diminished in more or less direct proportion to the frequency of the appearance of that image. We become dulled to it. Similarly, and as another component of this anaesthetic effect, the overwhelming presence and variety of images means that any image that disturbs, irritates or even invites thought and speculation, need not distract us for too long if disturbance, irritation or thought is held to be undesirable. The image is unable to force itself upon us. It cannot scar itself into our moral consciousness simply because it has to compete for attention with other images which are more attractive precisely because they are not so provoking.

Perhaps the most stimulating and entertaining reflection on all of these kinds of possibilities which can be held to be associated with the media (and, in the case of Andy Warhol, with art), is to be found in the work of Jean Baudrillard. Baudrillard is not just one of the most interesting commentators on the impact of the media on social, cultural and moral relationships, he is also one of the most peculiar. The peculiarity is due to Baudrillard's very odd and idiosyncratic prose style; nobody else writes sociology quite as he does (although his work has resulted in the appearance of a number of pale imitations). Indeed, there is often the hint that there might not be much more to what Baudrillard says *than* the style. It is this highly developed aesthetic sensibility that makes it extremely worthwhile to read Baudrillard's own words (or, rather, translations of Baudrillard's own words). Much of what he says might not make sense but, to some extent, that might well be exactly the point he is trying to make.

Baudrillard is very different to most other social and cultural commentators because he does not pretend that his work is necessarily right or even true. All he wants it to be is provocative. He sees himself as a 'theoretical terrorist', the terrorism residing in 'the savage tone and the subversive mentality' (Baudrillard 1993: 168). Moreover, Baudrillard is not interested in developing a sober and careful analysis of something conventionally called the 'real world'. Instead, he is more concerned to push ideas and logics to their very limits in order to attempt to provoke a response on the part of his reader. To this extent there is the very distinct possibility that a lot of what Baudrillard says is not meant to be taken entirely seriously. 'There is always an element of provocation in what I write. It is a sort of challenge to the intellectual and the reader that starts a kind of game' (Baudrillard 1993: 153–4). He might well say some of the things he says purely so that the reader can think for him- or herself exactly *why* this seems so silly. (Of course there is another, more cynical possibility; Baudrillard makes some deliberately dubious points to play a game at the expense of academia. Perhaps he is playing a game so that he can see how long it is before a silly idea becomes accepted as true by others.) Indeed, 'The secret of theory is that truth doesn't exist. You can't confront it in any way. The only thing you can do is play with some kind of provocative logic' (Baudrillard 1993: 124).

For all of these reasons it is a very questionable enterprise indeed to rehearse Baudrillard's arguments. It is difficult, if not actually utterly inappropriate, to take his ideas thoroughly seriously and to treat them as in any way definitive or final. But it is precisely because of these difficulties, because of this deeply yet playfully ironic stance which Baudrillard the intellectual adopts towards the products of Baudrillard the writer, that his work is actually worth discussing and considering. Baudrillard pushes themes and perspectives (and indeed the conventional narratives of sociological and cultural study) to their very limits. In so doing he proposes themes which others would reject as self-evidently ridiculous and throws many taken-for-granted beliefs and assumptions into very sharp relief. As such, it is perhaps best to realize that any attempt at a sober recounting of Baudrillard's work actually and almost necessarily serves to misrepresent it at least a little. It is certainly best to bear that caveat in mind with my discussion of Baudrillard.

Baudrillard is in little doubt that the media have had a thoroughly ironic effect and impact on social and cultural relationships. He writes pithily that, 'We are in a universe where there is more and more information, and less and less meaning' (Baudrillard 1983: 95). Indeed, Baudrillard goes on in a way that can be seen to parallel directly the conclusions reached when the attempt is made to understand whether the media can operate as channels of the communication of moral values and of the making of moral solidarity. Baudrillard also makes a point that can be applied almost directly to the ambivalences and the ambiguities of Warhol's *Jackie* when he suggests that 'information is directly destructive of meaning and signification, or neutralizes it. The loss of meaning is directly linked to the dissolving and dissuasive action of information, the media, and the mass media' (Baudrillard 1983: 96). Basically, Baudrillard is proposing that even though the media massively increase the amount of information that is available and in circulation (so that, for example, it is relatively easy through the press and television to get information about the famine in Ethiopia; moreover thanks to the narrative conventions of the media and the inability of any single individual actually to contradict the vast detail in any given news report, the media texts are invariably taken to be and are accepted as, in some way, mirrors of reality), the quality of that information – its ability to instantiate anything or to force any necessary meaning – tends to decline. Here it is possible to see the implication of connections between Baudrillard and Theodor Adorno; both draw some correlation between the increase of images or texts and the decrease of their value.

All of this leads Jean Baudrillard to a series of hypotheses which rather tend to stand some of the most sacred of sociological assumptions quite on their heads. Baudrillard is interested by the impact of the media's increase of information and texts on social and cultural relation-ships. He begins by quickly outlining the conventional approaches to this problem which are to be found in the works of sociology and sociologists. Baudrillard characterizes sociology as assuming that 'socialization is measured according to exposure through media messages. Those who are under-exposed to the media are virtually asocial or desocialized' (Baudrillard 1983: 96). Baudrillard is in little doubt that this is indeed a key assumption in analyses of the media: 'We are all accomplices in this myth. It is the alpha and omega of our modernity, without which the credibility of our social organization would collapse' (Baudrillard 1983: 97). It is exactly this 'myth' which Baudrillard upsets: 'Yet *the fact is that it* [i.e., our social organization] *is collapsing*. . . . Just where we think that information is producing meaning, it is doing the exact opposite' (Baudrillard 1983: 97).

Baudrillard's argument is that the media have caused both meaning (which for our purposes can be taken simply to refer to the ability of a text to instantiate) and for that matter the social, to disappear: 'Infor-mation devours its own contents; it devours communication and the social' (Baudrillard 1983: 97). According to Baudrillard it is possible to identify two reasons for and aspects of this odd situation.

Firstly, and in their own terms, the media operate so as to produce meaning; the media play the game of communication. But, for Baudrillard, the media actually exhaust themselves in this attempt to produce meaning. In order to illustrate this point, Baudrillard quickly stresses the significance of things such as viewer-participation pro-grammes on television; he suggests that with these programmes the audience becomes the event. As such, the media are able to produce meaning to the extent that they draw the audience into the creation of the media event. But, for Baudrillard, this appearance of meaning is actually chimerical. The hysterical participation means nothing other than itself. The meaning of the media event is, simply, the media event. Here, Baudrillard's arguments clearly reflect the impact of McLuhan's notion that 'the medium is the message'. According to Baudrillard, what pur-ports to be real participation is, instead, merely a *simulation* of partici-pation. 'More and more information is invaded by this sort of phantom content, this homeopathic graft, this awakened dream of communi-cation' (Baudrillard 1983: 98).

Baudrillard is saying that the media forms which uphold and which seem to increase the possibility of communication actually restrict and reduce the chance of real communication. On the one hand, communication is reduced to the level of whether or not the audience has something to say about the topics that are defined by the media as of concern. Meanwhile, and on the other hand, communication is only possible through the channels of the media. Anything else becomes redundant. Indeed, social and cultural relationships themselves tend to become little more than the things which are spoken about through the media. As a consequence of this, the channels of communication themselves seem to become all pervasive and all powerful. 'Thus communication as well as *the social* functions as a closed circuit, as a lure – to which is attached the force of a myth.' Baudrillard continues: 'The belief and the faith in information attached to this tautological proof give the system itself, by doubling its signs, an unlocatable reality' (Baudrillard 1983: 99).

Secondly, and extending out of the first point, Baudrillard proposes that 'Behind this exacerbated staging of communication, the mass media, with its pressure of information, carries out an irresistible destructuration of the social' (Baudrillard 1983: 100). Curiously, Baudrillard rather leaves unexplored and unexplained this aspect of his analysis of the impact of the media. All he says is that 'information dissolves meaning and the social into a sort of nebulous state leading not at all to a surfeit of innovation but to the very contrary, to total entropy' (Baudrillard 1983: 100). It is not readily apparent to a reader what this might mean.

When Baudrillard brings these two points together, he is in no doubt that it is possible to come to a very clear conclusion about the significance of the media. He ends up paraphrasing Marshall McLuhan once again. For Baudrillard, 'all the contents of meaning are absorbed in the dominant form of the medium. The medium alone makes the event – and does this whatever the contents, whether conformist or subversive' (Baudrillard 1983: 100). But Baudrillard wants to go further than McLuhan; the point is that when he proposed that 'the medium is the message', McLuhan still tended to assume some important distinction between the media themselves and the realities they represented. Certainly, in McLuhan's scheme the medium is the message but the occasion of the message has to come from outside (this is made clear by McLuhan's own discussion of the Kennedy assassination and, indeed, by an attempt to construct an analysis of Live Aid in the light of McLuhan's suggestions). Baudrillard rejects the validity of this orthodox belief that there is a difference of a fundamental and essential kind between the media and what they represent. He thinks that the distinction between the media and reality has been utterly and even irrevocably blurred to such an extent that it is quite impossible to know where the one ends and the other begins. Baudrillard talks about 'the implosion of the medium itself in the real, *the implosion of the medium and the real* in a sort of nebulous hyperreality where even the definition and the distinct action of the medium are no longer distinguishable' (Baudrillard 1983: 101).

The notion of hyperreality is important in the work of Baudrillard. It is also one way of understanding what he means when he refers to the implosion of meaning and of the social in the media. Conventionally, the media are understood as representing a reality which is to be found out there. That is to say, conventionally, it is understood that the media *refer* to something out there; that media texts have a *referent* (a thing to which they refer) in the real world. Furthermore, the text is here understood as something like a sign and an illusion of a real something else. The notion of hyperreality represents an attempt to define and come to terms with a situation in which this easy relationship between text and referent has been made problematic. Hyperreality 'is the disappearance of the referent – and it is in relation to this disappearance of the referent that there is a sort of omnipresence to the sign' (Baudrillard 1993: 142).

According to Baudrillard, one of the clearest examples of this hyper-reality is the political form of terrorism. He argues (and here it seems quite likely that Baudrillard is being wilfully provocative) that terrorism is not a form of political action that takes place in the 'real world'. Rather, Baudrillard sees terrorism as something that takes place purely in the hyperreal realm of the media; it is a symbol which means nothing other than itself. All meaning implodes when a terrorist bomb explodes. Moreover, he suggests that the media bring about the victory of the terrorists because they represent the event of the bomb going off but refuse to talk about whatever political motivation the terrorists might have had: 'And the media, all while orchestrating the victory of order, only cause the evidence for the opposite to reverberate: to wit, that terrorism is burying the political order' (Baudrillard 1983: 113).

Baudrillard goes on to develop his argument in a way that clearly demonstrates quite how provocative and mischievous he can be. He goes on to condemn the media and terrorism in the same breath: 'The media are terrorists in their own fashion, working continually to produce (good) sense, but, at the same time, violently defeating it by arousing everywhere a fascination without scruples' (Baudrillard 1983: 113–14). This 'fascination without scruples' is perhaps more or less the same emotion as Michael Ignatieff was trying to grasp, a lot more soberly, when he spoke about the voyeuristic dimension of the television pictures of famine and other forms of suffering. Terrorism is a form of hyperreality because, for Baudrillard, terrorism has no referent. It is, 'Not a real event, but a condensed narrative, a flash, a scenario – that is to say, that which opposes to every event said to be real the purest form of the spectacular' (Baudrillard 1983: 113–14). For Jean Baudrillard terrorism is, 'a ritual, or that which, of all possible events, opposes to the political and historical model or order the purest symbolic form of challenge' (Baudrillard 1983: 114). Like the media image it is, terrorism instantiates nothing apart from the challenge posed by terrorism.

Baudrillard seems to believe that terrorism cannot be understood and confronted all the time the media attempt precisely to understand it. He talks about 'the stupidity and the obscenity of all that is reported about the terrorists: everywhere the wish to palm off meaning on them, to exterminate them with meaning' (Baudrillard 1983: 117). However, Baudrillard goes on to make it plain that despite its provocations and playfulness his work does have a spine of moral seriousness: 'It is still this rage for meaning which makes us . . . treat them like idiots incapable of going all the way and blowing up the airplane and the passengers, which makes us want them not to have "won"' (Baudrillard 1983: 117). Despite the drift of some of his prose, it has to be said that Baudrillard never forgets that bombs *really* kill people.

In these terms, Andy Warhol's *Jackie* can also be interpreted in terms of the analysis of hyperreality in so far as it reflects the omnipresence of the sign of Jackie Kennedy to such an extent that it is quite unimportant who or what the 'real-life' Jackie might or might not have been. Indeed, Baudrillard says with the slightest hint of nostalgia for a lost (presumably real) social and cultural world that, 'With the advent of the media . . . we have lost that prior state of total illusion, of the sign as magic' (Baudrillard 1993: 143). Once again, *Jackie* possesses none of that aura of authenticity and none of that implication of a privileged connection to some reality which is able to make the painting actually mean something. The more information Andy Warhol presents about the face of Jackie Kennedy, the more meaning is made impossible. There is and can be no necessary instantiation.

With his reference to hyperreality, Baudrillard is trying to understand and present a situation in which all the taken-for-granted bases of meaning and action have been demolished. Indeed, '*the medium is the message* signifies not only the end of the message, but also the end of the medium' (Baudrillard 1983: 102). Baudrillard develops this point at somewhat greater length when he says that:

> There are no longer media in the literal sense of the term (I am talking above all about the electronic mass media) – that is to say, a power mediating between one reality and another, between one state of the

real and another – neither in content nor form. Strictly speaking, this is what implosion signifies: the absorption of one pole into another, the short-circuit between poles of every differential system of meaning, the effacement of terms and of distinct oppositions, and thus that of the medium and the real.

(Baudrillard 1983: 102–3)

With these kinds of comments, the terms of the analysis of the media have moved a very considerable way from the concerns and conclusions reached from within the confines of the narrative of cultural studies. Within cultural studies, of course, it is indeed assumed that there is an essential difference between the media on the one hand and the material world of everyday practices on the other hand. After all, it is precisely the assumption of this difference that makes it possible for cultural studies to investigate the media in terms of the problems of the constructions of hegemony and, for that matter, for cultural studies to revolve around the nothing which is yet something called popular culture.

But Baudrillard rejects the belief that it continues to be helpful to make sense of the world in terms of these kinds of fairly simple and simplistic polar oppositions. Instead, he collapses the media into the social and the social into the media so that to study the one is actually and of necessity to study the other. The notion of hyperreality is, for Baudrillard, a way of grasping the situation in which there is no difference, and no possibility of the identification of any kind of difference, between the media and the social. He is not averse to extending these social and cultural points into philosophical speculation and, indeed, neither is he too averse to adding the merest hint of conspiracy theory (although the latter is probably added simply for the sake of appearances):

Now the media are nothing else than a marvellous instrument for destabilizing the real and the true, all historical or political truth (there is thus no possible political strategy of the media: it is a contradiction in terms).

(Baudrillard 1988: 217)

Baudrillard once again sounds more than a little like Adorno when he concerns himself to talk about the nature of the audience of the media. Just as Adorno's monolithic category of the culture industry led him to identify a single passive audience which had been made barbaric, so Baudrillard also identifies a single and to all conventional appearances passive audience. However, Baudrillard replaces Adorno's concentration on the horror of barbarism with a critique of the loss of human responsibility for human being which owes very considerable debts to the legacy of French existentialism. Baudrillard believes that 'The large systems of information relieve the masses of the responsibility of having to know, to understand, to be informed, to be up on things' (Baudrillard 1993: 114). After all, within the imploded universe of hyperreality there actually is nothing to be up on, there is nothing to understand other than the media texts. There is nothing to be responsible *for* or *to*. More specifically: 'Advertising relieves people of the responsibility of having to choose, which is perfectly human and perfectly horrible' (Baudrillard 1993: 114). Advertising relieves me of the burden of choice because it has already made my choices for me; I know that if I buy a certain condom I will be a far more satisfying and thrilling sexual performer. Thus I am relieved of the difficulty of choosing from the chemist's cornucopia of condoms. As such, my life is less frightening, less bedevilled by the nagging fear that I have made the wrong choice; my life is less horrible. But, for all of that, it is also much less human.

Yet it is here that Adorno and Baudrillard begin to move apart very quickly indeed. Whereas Adorno sees the dehumanization of the audience as an affront not just to humanity but also to the promises of enlightenment, and whereas Adorno (with Max Horkheimer of course) connects this dehumanization with the rise of Nazism, Baudrillard sees the dehumanization as the basis of a negation of all of the appeals and the promises of the media. However, Baudrillard rejects the view that the negation of the media can be read simply as a kind of resistance. What Baudrillard identifies has absolutely nothing to do with the overtly political and organizational struggles of hegemony and popular culture which are so important within the narratives of cultural studies. Baudrillard sees the media as the basis and the site of an immensely different sort of the playing out of meanings and cultural relationships.

Baudrillard begins to develop an appreciation of the kinds of relationships that are generated around the media by stressing the widely held assumption that the media are involved in fundamentally dialogical relationships. This dialogue is generally taken to be one of rational communication. It is conventionally argued that the media broadcast or print a message which the audiences then respond to in some directly caused (and more or less immediately intelligible) way. As Baudrillard writes: 'Everywhere the masses are encouraged to speak, they are urged to live socially, electorally, organisationally, sexually, in participation, in festival, in free speech, etc.' (Baudrillard 1983: 23). Indeed he suggests that without this kind of rational dialogue, the whole social system would collapse.

According to Baudrillard, a passive and apathetic mass might well be desirable from the point of view 'characteristic of the bureaucratic and centralist phase of power' (Baudrillard 1983: 23). But contemporary forms of social organization and arrangement are, Baudrillard contends, predicated on the active participation of the masses. Writing of the strategies of power he suggests: 'That is why it seeks to reverse its strategies: from passivity to participation, from silence to speech' (Baudrillard 1983: 23). In these terms, then, the dialogical form of media texts would be identified as one way in which the dominated social groups can be forced to participate in social and cultural relationships. Through the requirements of the kinds of dialogue which the media can create and allow, the subordinated social groups (the objects towards which power is directed) can be forced to have a stake in the status quo. (It is noticeable that these points by Baudrillard are not too far removed from Gramsci's analytic of hegemony. Certainly, the prose styles of Antonio Gramsci and Jean Baudrillard are astonishingly different, but perhaps the actual points they are trying to make are not as dissimilar as first impressions might lead one to think.)

Baudrillard is in no doubt that the media try to create a series of dialogues between texts and the masses (that is, in a different guise, with audiences), because otherwise the social stability of the masses could not be taken for granted. Here, then, Baudrillard is using for his own purposes the conventional sociological story that the media socialize individuals and groups. Baudrillard uses it to reveal the conceits of, and launch an assault on, the orthodox interpretations of what it is that the media do and are for. He begins by outlining, in what can only be seen as almost crassly conspiratorial terms, the major aim which the media attribute to themselves: 'Whatever its political, pedagogical, cultural content, the plan is always to get some meaning across, to keep the masses *within reason*' (Baudrillard 1983: 9). This urge and almost panic-stricken enterprise of keeping the 'masses within reason' is 'an imperative to produce meaning that takes the form of the constantly repeated imperative to moralise information: to better inform, to better socialise, to raise the cultural level of the masses, etc.' (Baudrillard 1983: 9–10).

It is at this point that Baudrillard becomes able to outline the nature of the responses on the part of the masses towards the media. The responses essentially involve a refusal to participate in the dialogic relationships; a refusal to participate in the webs and the relationships of *meaning*. According to Baudrillard, the masses refuse to be brought within the bounds of reason. He states that 'the masses scandalously

resist this imperative of rational communication. They are given meaning: they want spectacle' (Baudrillard 1983: 10). Baudrillard sees this
refusal of meaning, this refusal to participate in the dialogues which the
media promote, as an extremely active strategy on the part of the
masses. He argues that even though people sit in front of their television
screens and get bored if the programme is not exciting, it would be
utterly wrong to argue therefore that the audiences have been duped by
the media so that they are now all but brain-dead (and most certainly
socially and politically quiet).

For Baudrillard the fact that audiences watch television and only get
bored, watch television and refuse to accept the claims of the broad-
casters that the programmes are true or interesting, amounts to a positive
strategic decision. The masses are not quiet because they have been
stunned: 'it is not a question of mystification: it is a question of their
own exigencies, of an explicit and positive counter-strategy – the task of
absorbing and annihilating culture, knowledge, power, the social'
(Baudrillard 1983: 11). To pretend otherwise, to pretend that the media
audiences have indeed been mystified is merely intellectual arrogance.
According to Baudrillard nothing is 'served by alleging that they are
mystified. This is always a hypocritical hypothesis which protects the
intellectual complaisance of the producers of meaning: the masses spontaneously aspire to the natural light of reason' (Baudrillard 1983: 10).
Basically, Baudrillard is saying that there is no reason at all to presuppose that the masses want to live in the brightness of enlightenment;
it might well be more helpful to suppose that the masses just want to be
entertained before they die.

In order to illustrate these points, Baudrillard discusses an incident in
France. On the night that a political militant was extradited from France
to Germany, France was playing in a televised football match to qualify
for the World Cup finals. Baudrillard portrays the night in the following
way: 'Some hundreds of people demonstrated outside la Sante, a few
barristers ran to and fro in the night; twenty million people spent their
evening glued to the screen.' There was: 'An explosion of popular joy
when France won. Consternation and indignation of the illuminati over
this scandalous indifference' (Baudrillard 1983: 12). The consternation
which Baudrillard attributes to the French intelligentsia, who simply
could not understand why a goal in a football match generated a greater
response than an important question of civil liberties, had been felt many
years earlier in 1930s Britain by George Orwell.

In *The Road to Wigan Pier*, Orwell wrote a passage which illustrates
almost perfectly the kind of point Baudrillard is trying to make about

how the intelligentsia (mis)understand the activities of the masses and, more specifically, media audiences. Orwell begins by drawing parallels between how people respond to political events and football-related incidents, and then he develops a full moral and political critique of the media. Orwell writes:

> I happened to be in Yorkshire when Hitler re-occupied the Rhineland. Hitler, Locarno, Fascism, and the threat of war aroused hardly a flicker of interest locally, but the decision of the Football Association to stop publishing their fixtures in advance (this was an attempt to quell the Football Pools) flung all Yorkshire into a storm of fury. And then there is the queer spectacle of modern electrical science showering miracles upon people with empty bellies. . . . Twenty million people are underfed but literally everyone in England has access to radio. What we have lost in food we have gained in electricity.
>
> (Orwell 1962: 80)

Clearly, Orwell thinks that it is a political and a moral outrage that the expansionism of Hitler's Germany should cause less outrage than the question of whether or not football fixtures should be published in advance. He sees these responses as out of proportion to the events which caused them and lays the blame for this situation firmly in the lap of the media. For Orwell, the media have caused their audiences to make trivial things vital and vital things trivial. According to Orwell, this situation prevails to such an extent that people no longer care about their diet so long as they are being entertained: 'Whole sections of the working class who have been plundered of all they really need are being compensated, in part, by cheap luxuries which mitigate the surface of life' (Orwell 1962: 80).

Orwell's response to the perspectives on the world of the working class of Yorkshire rests on two key assumptions. Firstly, Orwell assumes that the media are in some way responsible for the manipulation of the working class so that they are distracted from the really important and pressing issues (such as fascism and food) by a combination of advertising and football. Secondly, and this is what drives Orwell's prose, he assumes that the intellectual has a duty to reveal the absurdities of this situation; a duty to express disgust and outrage. In both cases, Orwell rather sees the media audiences as the witless dupes of the press and the radio; he fails to understand why they do what they do and wraps up that lack of understanding in a cloak of moral despair.

Baudrillard rejects this kind of argument because it fails to see any possibility that the indifference of the masses towards what are said to be the great issues of the day might actually be a rather positive thing. Baudrillard points to the nub of the intellectuals' method of trying to understand how and why football is popularly preferred over politics: 'One same reason is invoked: the manipulation of the masses by power, their mystification by football' (Baudrillard 1983: 12). He continues to show why there is this indifference on the part of the commentators towards the *reasons* for these preferences (after all, all the intellectuals do is express their outrage; they do not seek to understand): 'In any case, this indifference *ought* not to be, hence it has nothing to tell us . . . the "silent majority" is even stripped of its indifference, it has no right even that this be recognised and imputed to it' (Baudrillard 1983: 12–13).

It is precisely this indifference that Baudrillard wants to emphasize. He sees it as the basis of the masses' strategy of the negation of the attempt of the media to communicate meanings. Like George Orwell, the media operate on the assumption that the masses (that is, the audiences), respond to the meanings which are communicated to them. In other words, the dialogue between media texts and media audiences is taken to be essentially rational so that there ought to prevail a situation in which the most pressing issues generate the greatest response (or, more conspiratorially, the most trivial issues will generate the greatest response if that means that the existing relationships of power can remain intact). It is assumed that the masses will take meaning into themselves and then create yet more meanings so that the relationships between the media and their audiences are a perpetual ebb and flow of information. Within the parameters of these kinds of assumptions, the fact that the audiences do not respond to the meanings of momentous political events is thus the product of either conspiracy or stupidity. But for Baudrillard the unresponsiveness of the masses is a positive political strategy.

The media want the masses to participate in social and cultural activity; it is precisely this participation in rationality that the masses reject. Instead, all they uphold is the appeal of the exciting spectacle. According to Baudrillard: 'The mass absorbs all the social energy, but no longer refracts it. It absorbs every sign and every meaning, but no longer reflects them. It absorbs all messages and digests them' (Baudrillard 1983: 28). In other words, the masses take in everything the media give them, but then they resolutely refuse to participate in the dialogues which the media require. And so the media respond with desperation; they communicate ever more frantically the messages of social participation only for those messages to meet with ever greater silence. The masses consequently negate the ability of the media to carry out any kind of communication.

Baudrillard appears to be in no doubt that this collapse of the dialogues which hold together the webs of social relationships has to be understood as a political conflict. But it is not the kind of politics where the masses have the responsibility to speak to and on behalf of grand universal constituencies such as the oppressed of the world. Quite the contrary, it is a politics in which the masses refuse the responsibilities which the struggle to impose meanings tries to force upon them (for Baudrillard the masses actually refuse the responsibility of bearing the meaning of oppression or for that matter of anything else). He argues that political rationality only continues to survive because of 'a credibility hypothesis' which is built around the assumption of dialogue. The 'credibility hypothesis' states that, 'the masses are permeable to action and to discourse, that they hold an opinion, that they are present behind all the surveys and statistics' (Baudrillard 1983: 37). But, Baudrillard says, in the desperate attempt to communicate meanings, the media have represented politics through the conventions of game shows; and so the masses treat politics as if it was as important as a television game show: 'For some time now, the electoral game has been akin to TV game shows in the consciousness of the people'. Consequently the masses 'who have always served as alibi and as supernumerary on the political stage, avenge themselves by treating as a *theatrical* performance the political scene and its actors' (Baudrillard 1983: 37). Baudrillard continues:

> At no time are the masses politically or historically engaged in a conscious manner. . . . Nor is this a flight from politics, but rather the effect of an implacable antagonism between the class (caste?) which bears the social the political, culture – master of time and history, and the un(in)formed, residual, senseless mass. The former continually seeks to perfect the reign of meaning, to invest, to saturate the field of the social, the other continually distorts every effect of meaning, neutralises or diminishes them.
>
> (Baudrillard 1983: 38)

Basically, then, Baudrillard is building his analysis on a similar definition of culture to that which was used by Tony Bennett; culture is the creation and use of meanings. Baudrillard extends this definition so that it also encompasses politics and society itself. But for Baudrillard the communication of meanings collapses. The meanings which are directed towards the masses are refused by the masses who, instead, only concern themselves with spectacles (such as football matches) which instantiate nothing necessary. By extension this means that the dialogues which even Baudrillard is prepared to see as the normal basis of social and cultural activity are turned into a monologue. And just as Voloshinov says that a lecture is impossible if it becomes a monologue, so Baudrillard says that society (and even culture) becomes impossible if it becomes an entirely one-way flow.

In Baudrillard's world, all that are left are the fleeting appearances of the media spectacles. In themselves, these spectacles mean nothing; they lack all responsibility and cannot possibly be the occasion for imaginations of moral responsibility. Baudrillard sees only, 'neutralization of every message in a vacuous ether' (Baudrillard 1983: 35). This is a large-scale version of the world of the ambiguities, ambivalences and ultimate lack of humanity which is represented so well in Andy Warhol's paintings of Jackie Kennedy; a world which might seem to be one of sorrow but which cannot force sorrow upon us.

In these terms, social and cultural values cannot be communicated because they are either the useless appendages of spectacles or, and in Baudrillard's terms this is far more likely, they cannot be communicated because that communication would entail a dialogue which the masses would refuse. As such, in the moment of their communication any cultural or moral values that certain products or activities might possess would be fated to wither and die. The responsibility of a dialogue would be smashed against the hard face of the monologue.

The logical consequence of the narrative I have been developing is the argument that, thanks to the media and especially thanks to the tendency towards the destruction of the ability of images to have an authority and integrity in and of themselves, cultural and moral values can only survive if they remain more or less entirely personal affairs (or if, at the very most, they are confined within the exclusive boundaries of fairly restricted 'aesthetic communities'). Perhaps, in these terms, the best way of defending cultural and moral values is precisely to keep them outside of the dialogues and meanings of the media. But that kind of a defence would be utterly ironic. It would be to defend the importance of culture and morality whilst denying their significance. In making values matter *to me*, I will be paying the price of not being able to make them matter to anybody else.

It would also mean that media texts and images would be consigned for ever to an inability to act as channels of the communication of the values of moral solidarity. After all, if something is valuable purely to the extent that it matters to me, then there is absolutely no way in which it will be possible to break out of the boundaries of this thoroughly private language of worth. There will be no way in which my definitions and determinations of value might act as tools for the transcendence of the existing barriers between us and them. Certainly, *I* might be able to imagine similarities between me and the famished inhabitants of Ethiopia or the suffering widow, but there would be absolutely no way in which I might communicate my leaps of the moral imagination to you. And so moral solidarity would be a contradiction in terms. Where there should be endless dialogue, debate and dispute there is and probably will remain only silence.

The media will not, because they cannot, act as channels of the communication of value. The speculative and deep questions of value are utterly incompatible with the tendencies of the media towards spectacular and endlessly reproducible texts which instantiate absolutely nothing. When all is said and done, Live Aid did not change the world; people still starve to death although a few credit-card holders in Britain and America might be able to sleep a little easier in their beds under their 'ethnic' duvet covers. Certainly the media communicate harrowing representations of others, but the more the face of the other is communicated and reproduced in this way the more it is denuded of any of the moral authority it might otherwise possess. Increased visibility to the gaze seems to go hand in hand with increasing invisibility from the point of view of the responsibility of moral solidarity. Media significance means moral insignificance. The image of the other, and therefore the face of the other, which should be so compelling according to Levinas and Sontag, becomes commonplace and incapable of attracting a thoughtful or deliberate second glance. Even less is it capable of *demanding* any kind of a second thought. That is one of the terrible things which Andy Warhol shows so well. In seeing *Jackie*, Jackie is forgotten.

Bibliography

Adorno, Theodor 1974 'The Stars Down to Earth: The Los Angeles Times Astrology Column', *Telos*, 19: 13–90.

—— 1989 'Perennial Fashion – Jazz', in S.E. Bonner and D.M. Kellner (eds), *Critical Theory and Society. A Reader*, New York: Routledge.

—— 1991 *The Culture Industry. Selected Essays on Mass Culture*, ed. J.M. Bernstein, London: Routledge.

Adorno, Theodor and Horkheimer, Max 1972 *Dialectic of Enlightenment*, trans. J. Cumming, New York: Herder and Herder.

Bachrach, Peter and Baratz, Morton S. 1970 *Power and Poverty. Theory and Practice*, New York: Oxford University Press.

Baudrillard, Jean 1983 *In the Shadow of the Silent Majorities . . . Or the End of the Social*, trans. P. Foss, P. Patton and J. Johnston, New York: Semiotext(e).

—— 1988 *Selected Writings*, ed. M. Poster, Cambridge: Polity.

—— 1993 *Baudrillard Live. Selected Interviews*, ed. M. Gane, London: Routledge.

Bauman, Zygmunt 1990 *Thinking Sociologically*, Oxford: Blackwell.

Benjamin, Walter 1973 *Illuminations*, trans. H. Zohn, London: Fontana.

Bennett, Tony 1980 'Popular Culture: A "Teaching Object"', *Screen Education* 34: 17–29.

—— 1981 *Popular Culture: Themes and Issues (1)*, Milton Keynes: The Open University Press.

—— 1981a *Popular Culture: Themes and Issues (2)*, Milton Keynes: The Open University Press.

—— 1986 'Introduction: Popular Culture and "The Turn to Gramsci"', in T. Bennett, C. Mercer and J. Woollacott (eds), *Popular Culture and Social Relations*, Milton Keynes: The Open University Press.

—— 1986a 'The Politics of the "Popular" and Popular Culture', in T. Bennett, C. Mercer and J. Woollacott (eds), *Popular Culture and Social Relations*, Milton Keynes: The Open University Press.

Berger, John 1972 *Ways of Seeing*, Harmondsworth: Penguin.

Buck-Morss, Susan 1977 *The Origin of Negative Dialectics. Theodor W. Adorno, Walter Benjamin, and the Frankfurt School*, New York: The Free Press.

Cohen, Stanley 1972 *Folk Devils and Moral Panics. The Creation of the Mods and Rockers*, London: MacGibbon & Kee.

Coplans, John n.d. *Andy Warhol*, London: Weidenfeld & Nicolson.

Elias, Norbert 1978 *The History of Manners. The Civilizing Process Volume 1*, trans. E. Jephcott, Oxford: Basil Blackwell.

Engels, Frederick 1942 'Speech at the Graveside of Karl Marx', in *Karl Marx. Selected Works in Two Volumes*, vol. 1, London: Lawrence & Wishart.

Fetterman, David M. 1989 *Ethnography. Step by Step*, Applied Social Research Methods Series Volume 17, Newbury Park: Sage.

Fiske, John 1987 *Television Culture*, London: Methuen.

—— 1989 *Understanding Popular Culture*, London: Unwin Hyman.

—— 1992 'Cultural Studies and the Culture of Everyday Life', in L. Grossberg, C. Nelson and P.A. Treichler, *Cultural Studies*, New York: Routledge.

Frankfurt Institute for Social Research 1973 *Aspects of Sociology*, trans, J. Viertel, London: Heinemann Educational Books.

Gilroy, Paul 1982 'Steppin' out of Babylon – Race, Class and Autonomy', in Centre for Contemporary Cultural Studies, *The Empire Strikes Back. Race and Racism in 70s Britain*, London: Hutchinson.

Gramsci, Antonio 1971 *Selections from the Prison Notebooks*, ed. and trans. Q. Hoare and G. Nowell Smith, London: Lawrence & Wishart.

Hall, Stuart 1980 'Cultural Studies and the Centre: Some Problematics and Problems', in S. Hall *et al.* (eds), *Culture, Media, Language. Working Papers in Cultural Studies, 1972–79*, London: Hutchinson.

—— 1986 'Introduction' in D. Morley, *Family Television. Cultural Power and Domestic Leisure*, London: Comedia/Routledge.

—— 1990 'The Emergence of Cultural Studies and the Crisis of the Humanities', *October*, 53: 11–90.

—— 1992 'Cultural Studies and its Theoretical Legacies', in L. Grossberg, C. Nelson and P. Treichler (eds), *Cultural Studies*, New York: Routledge.

Hall, Stuart; Critcher, Chas; Jefferson, Tony; *et al.* 1978 *Policing the Crisis: Mugging, the State and Law and Order*, London: Macmillan.

Hall, Stuart and Jacques, Martin (eds) 1989 *New Times*, London: Lawrence & Wishart.

Heidegger, Martin 1962 *Being and Time*, trans J. Macquarie and E. Robinson, New York: Harper & Row.

Hobson, Dorothy 1980 'Housewives and the Mass Media', in S. Hall *et al.* (eds), *Culture, Media, Language. Working Papers in Cultural Studies, 1972–79*, London: Hutchinson.

Hoggart, Richard 1958 *The Uses of Literacy*, Penguin: Harmondsworth.

Horkheimer, Max 1972 *Critical Theory*, New York: Herder & Herder.

Huband, Mark 1993 'War Games', *Guardian Weekend*, 9 January: 14–15, 38.

Ignatieff, Michael 1985 'Is Nothing Sacred? The Ethics of Television', *Daedalus*, 114(4): 57–78.

Inglis, Fred 1990 *Media Theory. An Introduction*, Oxford: Basil Blackwell.

Jensen, Klaus Bruhn 1992 'The Politics of Polysemy: Television News, Everyday Consciousness and Political Action', in P. Scannell, P. Schlesinger and C. Sparks (eds), *Culture and Power. A Media, Culture and Society Reader*, London: Sage.

Kant, Immanuel 1970 'An Answer to the Question: What is Enlightenment?' in H. Reiss (ed.), *Kant's Political Writings*, Cambridge: Cambridge University Press.

Lash, Scott 1990 'Learning from Leipzig – Or Politics in the Semiotic Society', *Theory, Culture and Society*, 7(4): 145–58.

Lawrence, Errol 1982 'Just Plain Common Sense: the "Roots" of Racism', in Centre for Contemporary Cultural Studies, *The Empire Strikes Back. Race and Racism in 70s Britain*, London: Hutchinson.

Levinas, Emmanuel 1988 *The Provocation of Levinas. Rethinking the Other*, ed. R. Bernasconi and D. Wood, London: Routledge.

Live Aid 1985 *Live Aid* Concert Programme, London.

McLuhan, Marshall 1964 *Understanding Media. The Extensions of Man*, London: Routledge & Kegan Paul.

McLuhan, Marshall and Powers, B. 1989 *The Global Village*, New York: Oxford University Press.

Malcolmson, Robert 1982 'Popular Recreations Under Attack', in B. Waites, T. Bennett and G. Martin (eds), *Popular Culture: Past and Present*, London: Croom Helm.

Marx, Karl 1938 *Capital. A Critical Analysis of Capitalist Production*, vol. 1, London: George Allen & Unwin.

—— 1946 'Theses on Feuerbach', in F. Engels, *Ludwig Feuerbach and the End of Classical German Philosophy*, Moscow: Progress Publishers.

Marx, Karl and Engels, Frederick 1970 *The German Ideology*, ed. C.J. Arthur, London: Lawrence & Wishart.

Mills, C. Wright 1959 *The Sociological Imagination*, New York: Oxford University Press.

Modleski, Tania 1984 *Loving With a Vengeance: Mass-Produced Fantasies for Women*, London: Methuen.

Morley, David 1986 *Family Television. Cultural Power and Domestic Leisure*, London: Comedia/Routledge.

Morphet, Richard 1971 'Andy Warhol', in *Warhol. The Tate Gallery 17 February–28 March 1971*, London: The Tate Gallery.

Orwell, George 1962 *The Road to Wigan Pier*, Harmondsworth: Penguin.

Rorty, Richard 1989 *Contingency, Irony, and Solidarity*, Cambridge: Cambridge University Press.

Savage, Jon 1991 *England's Dreaming. Sex Pistols and Punk Rock*, London: Faber & Faber.

Shanes, Eric 1991 *Warhol*, London: Studio Editions.

Solomos, John; Findlay, Bob; Jones, Simon and Gilroy, Paul 1982 'The Organic Crisis of British Capitalism and Race: the Experience of the Seventies', in Centre for Contemporary Cultural Studies, *The Empire Strikes Back. Race and Racism in 70s Britain*, London: Hutchinson.

Sontag, Susan 1991 *Illness as Metaphor and AIDS and its Metaphors*, Harmondsworth: Penguin.

Stein, Jean 1982 *Edie. An American Biography*, edited with G. Plimpton, New York: Dell.

Steiner, George 1989 *Real Presences*, London: Faber & Faber.

Summers, Anthony 1985 *Goddess. The Secret Lives of Marilyn Monroe*, London: Victor Gollancz.

Tetzlaff, David 1992 'Popular Culture and Social Control in Late Capitalism', in P. Scannell, P. Schlesinger and C. Sparks (eds), *Culture and Power. A Media, Culture and Society Reader*, London: Sage.

Voloshinov, V.N. 1988 'The Construction of the Utterance', trans. N. Owen, in A. Shukman (ed.), *Bakhtin School Papers*, Colchester: Russian Poetics in Translation Publications.

Weber, Max 1930 *The Protestant Ethic and the Spirit of Capitalism*, trans. T. Parsons, London: George Allen & Unwin.

Willis, Paul 1977 *Learning to Labour: How Working Class Kids Get Working Class Jobs*, Farnborough: Saxon House.

Zweig, Stefan 1943 *The World of Yesterday*, London: Cassell.

Name index

Adorno, T. 6, 34–45, 46, 47, 48,
  49–55, 57, 58, 59–63, 64, 65, 66,
  67, 70–1, 75, 76, 77–8, 79, 81, 82,
  100, 107, 115, 117, 122, 123

Bachrach, P. 103–4
Bakhtin, M. 58
Baratz, M. 103–4
Baudrillard, J. 7, 116–29
Bauman, Z. 5
Benjamin, W. 45–8, 52–3, 115
Bennett, T. 12–17, 20, 23, 24, 25,
  30, 38, 59, 115, 128
Berger, J. 48–9, 52–3

Cage, J. 111
Cohen, S. 83–4, 85
Coplans, J. 111–12

Elias, N. 13, 31
Engels, F. 67

Fetterman, D. 71–2
Fiske, J. 25, 67–71, 75, 77–8, 93

Gilroy, P. 19–20, 22–3
Gramsci, A. 10, 16, 17–19, 21–2, 27,
  124

Hall, S. 4, 12, 21, 22, 24, 25, 59, 75,
  84–5, 115
Heidegger, M. 5, 78
Hobson, D. 72–3, 74, 99
Hoggart, R. 4, 10, 63–6, 82
Horkheimer, M. 6, 34–5, 37–40, 41,

49, 54, 57, 58, 59–63, 64, 65, 66,
  67, 70–1, 75, 76, 77–8, 79, 82,
  100, 123

Huband, M. 88

Ignatieff, M. 89–90, 92, 93, 94–7,
  98, 100, 101, 104, 108, 120
Inglis, F. 75

Jensen, K. B. 69, 98–100, 101, 104

Kant, I. 49, 51
Kennedy, J. 7, 109–15, 121, 129–30

Lash, S. 61
Lawrence, E. 27

Marx, K. 16, 17, 34, 67, 76
McLuhan, M. 86, 87–9, 90, 118, 119
Mills, C. W. 5
Modleski, T. 73, 74, 99
Monroe, M. 60
Morley, D. 73–9, 81, 98, 99
Morphet, R. 112, 114
Musil, R. 1

Orwell, G. 64, 125–6, 127

Poe, E. A. 31

Rorty, R. 6–7, 90–2, 93, 96, 97, 101,
  103, 104, 107–10, 111, 114

Tetzlaff, D. 71

Subject index